P9-DFW-094

Designing & Assessing Educational Objectives

Robert J. Marzano
John S. Kendall

Designing &Assessing Educational Objectives

Applying the
New Taxonomy

A Joint Publication

NATIONAL ASSOCIATION OF ELEMENTARY SCHOOL PRINCIPALS
Serving All Elementary and Middle Level Principals

NATIONAL ASSOCIATION OF SECONDARY SCHOOL PRINCIPALS
promoting excellence in middle and high school leadership

CORWIN PRESS
A SAGE Company
Thousand Oaks, CA 91320

For information:

Corwin Press
A SAGE Company
2455 Teller Road
Thousand Oaks, California 91320
www.corwinpress.com

SAGE Pvt. Ltd.
B 1/I 1 Mohan Cooperative
  Industrial Area
Mathura Road, New Delhi 110 044
India

SAGE Ltd.
1 Oliver's Yard
55 City Road
London EC1Y 1SP
United Kingdom

SAGE Asia-Pacific Pte. Ltd.
33 Pekin Street #02-01
Far East Square
Singapore 048763

Printed in the United States of America.

Library of Congress Cataloging-in-Publication Data

Marzano, Robert J.
Designing and assessing educational objectives : applying the new taxonomy/by Robert J. Marzano and John S. Kendall.
    p. cm.
A joint publication with the American Association of School Administrators, the National Association of Elementary School Principals, and the National Association of Secondary School Principals.
Includes bibliographical references and index.
ISBN 978-1-4129-4034-4 (cloth)
ISBN 978-1-4129-4035-1 (pbk.)
    1. Education—Aims and objectives—Evaluation. I. Kendall, John S. II. Title.

LB17.M393 2008
370.11—dc22   2007050194

This book is printed on acid-free paper.

08   09   10   11   12   10 9 8 7 6 5 4 3 2

Acquisitions Editor:	Dan Alpert
Editorial Assistant:	Tatiana Richards
Production Editor:	Veronica Stapleton
Copy Editor:	Marilyn Power Scott
Typesetter:	C&M Digitals (P) Ltd.
Proofreader:	Caryne Brown
Indexer:	Kathy Paparchontis
Cover Designer:	Monique Hahn

Contents

About the Authors

Dr. Robert J. Marzano is President and founder of Marzano & Associates in Centennial, Colorado, Senior Scholar at Mid-continent Research for Education and Learning (McREL) in Aurora, Colorado, and Associate Professor at Cardinal Stritch University in Milwaukee, Wisconsin. He is the author of 30 books, 150 articles and chapters in books, and 100 sets of curriculum materials for teachers and students in Grades K–12. His works include *The New Taxonomy of Educational Objectives, What Works in Schools: Translating Research Into Action, School Leadership That Works, Building Background Knowledge for Academic Achievement, Classroom Management That Works, Classroom Instruction That Works, Classroom Assessment and Grading That Work,* and *The Art and Science of Teaching.*

During his forty years in public education, Marzano has worked multiple times in every state as well as in a host of countries in Europe and Asia. The central theme in his work has been translating research and theory into practical programs and tools for K–12 teachers and administrators.

John S. Kendall is a Senior Director in research at McREL. There he directs a technical assistance unit that develops and provides standards-related services for schools, districts, states, and other organizations. Clients have included Achieve, Inc., The College Board, and NASA's Jet Propulsion Lab. He has been with McREL seventeen years as Research Assistant, Program Associate, and Senior Director.

An internationally recognized expert in the development and improvement of standards for education, Kendall has consulted for more than fifty school districts and fourteen state departments of education as well as education agencies in the U.S. territories and abroad. Senior author of *Content Knowledge: A Compendium of Standards and Benchmarks for K–12 Education,* he has authored or coauthored six books and more than thirty monographs, technical studies, and articles. He received his undergraduate and master's degrees from the University of Colorado at Boulder.

Kendall's current research and technical assistance efforts include working with clients to establish performance standards for the classroom, developing standards for principals, and identifying the knowledge and skills that help students learn.

CHAPTER ONE

A New Perspective on Educational Objectives

This handbook is a guide to the design and assessment of educational objectives. It is a practical application of *The New Taxonomy of Educational Objectives* (Marzano & Kendall, 2007). While the New Taxonomy has a number of potential uses, here we focus on designing and assessing educational objectives. As indicated by its title, The New Taxonomy is designed as a replacement for Bloom et al.'s taxonomy, published in 1956 (Bloom, Englehart, Furst, Hill, & Krathwohl, 1956) Although that work was powerful and enduring, it had some flaws and inconsistencies that can now be reconciled, given the sixty-plus years of research and theory since its publication (for a detailed discussion, see Marzano & Kendall, 2007).

Bloom's taxonomy made a major contribution to the science of designing educational objectives. Indeed, prior to its publication, there was not much agreement as to the nature of objectives. Bloom adopted Ralph Tyler's (Airasian, 1994) notion that an educational objective should contain a clear reference to a specific type of knowledge as well as the behaviors that would signal understanding or skill related to that knowledge.

Like Bloom's taxonomy and others based on it (e.g., Anderson et al., 2001), the New Taxonomy has a specific syntax for educational objectives. We use the following stem for all objectives: *The student (or students) will be able to . . .* plus a verb phrase and an object. The verb phrase states the mental process that is to be employed while completing the objective, and the object is the knowledge that is the focus of the objective.

The New Taxonomy can be represented as depicted in Figure 1.1. The rows on the left-hand side of Figure 1.1 represent three systems of thought and in the case of the cognitive system, four subcomponents of that system. The columns on the right-hand side of Figure 1.1 depict three different types or domains of

Figure 1.1   The New Taxonomy

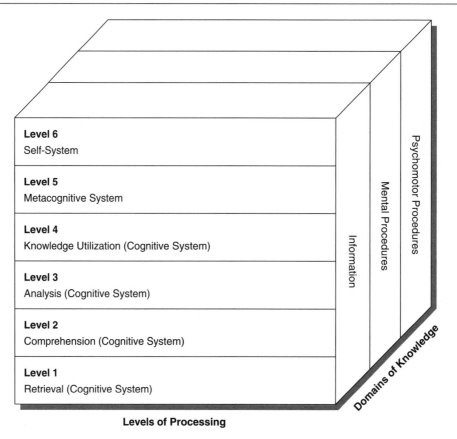

Source: Marzano & Kendall (2007)

knowledge: information, mental procedures, and psychomotor procedures. In effect, the New Taxonomy is two-dimensional. One dimension addresses three domains of knowledge; the other addresses levels of mental processing.

One of the defining differences between Bloom's taxonomy and the New Taxonomy is that the New Taxonomy separates various types of knowledge from the mental processes that operate on them. This is depicted in Figure 1.2.

As shown in Figure 1.2, Bloom included knowledge as a component of his taxonomy. About this, Bloom and his colleagues (1956) noted,

> By knowledge, we mean that the student can give evidence that he remembers either by recalling or by recognizing some idea or phenomenon with which he has had experience in the educational process. For our taxonomy purposes, we are defining knowledge as little more than the remembering of the idea or phenomenon in a form very close to that in which it was originally encountered. (pp. 28–29)

Figure 1.2   Knowledge as Addressed in the Two Taxonomies

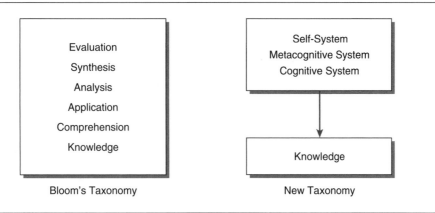

Source: Marzano & Kendall (2007)

On the other hand, Bloom identified specific types of knowledge within the knowledge category. These included

Terminology

Specific facts

Conventions

Trends or sequences

Classifications and categories

Criteria

Methodology

Principles and generalizations

Theories and structures

Thus within his knowledge category, Bloom included various forms of knowledge as well as the ability to recall and recognize that knowledge. This mixing of types of knowledge with the various mental operations that act on knowledge is one of the major weaknesses of Bloom's Taxonomy since it confuses the object of an action with the action itself. The New Taxonomy avoids this confusion by postulating three domains of knowledge that are operated on by the three systems of thought and their component elements. It is the systems of thought that have the hierarchical structure that constitutes the New Taxonomy.

We consider the specifics of the New Taxonomy in Chapter 2. Here we briefly introduce the framework to demonstrate the nature and format of the educational objectives that can be designed and assessed using it. To illustrate, consider Figure 1.3.

Figure 1.3   General Form of Educational Objectives for Each Level of the New Taxonomy

New Taxonomy Level	Operation	General Form of Objectives
Level 6: Self-System Thinking	Examining Importance	The student will be able to identify how important the information, mental procedure, or psychomotor procedure is to him or her and the reasoning underlying this perception.
	Examining Efficacy	The student will be able to identify beliefs about his or her ability to improve competence or understanding relative to the information, mental procedure, or psychomotor procedure and the reasoning underlying this perception.
	Examining Emotional Response	The student will be able to identify his or her emotional responses to the information, mental procedure, or psychomotor procedure and the reasons for these responses.
	Examining Motivation	The student will be able to identify his or her overall level of motivation to improve competence or understanding relative to the information, mental procedure, or psychomotor procedure and the reasons for this level of motivation.
Level 5: Metacognition	Specifying Goals	The student will be able to establish a goal relative to the information, mental procedure, or psychomotor procedure and a plan for accomplishing that goal.
	Process Monitoring	The student will be able to monitor progress toward the accomplishment of a specific goal relative to the information, mental procedure, or psychomotor procedure.
	Monitoring Clarity	The student will be able to determine the extent to which he or she has clarity about the information, mental procedure, or psychomotor procedure.
	Monitoring Accuracy	The student will be able to determine the extent to which he or she is accurate about the information, mental procedure, or psychomotor procedure.
Level 4: Knowledge Utilization	Decision Making	The student will be able to use the information, mental procedure, or psychomotor procedure to make decisions in general or make decisions about the use of the information, mental procedure, or psychomotor procedure.
	Problem Solving	The student will be able to use the information, mental procedure, or psychomotor procedure to solve problems in general or solve problems about the information, mental procedure, or psychomotor procedure.
	Experimenting	The student will be able to use the information, mental procedure, or psychomotor procedure to generate and test hypotheses in general or generate and test hypotheses about the information, mental procedure, or psychomotor procedure.

New Taxonomy Level	Operation	General Form of Objectives
	Investigating	The student will be able to use the information, mental procedure, or psychomotor procedure to conduct investigations in general or conduct investigations about the information, mental procedure, or psychomotor procedure.
Level 3: Analysis	Matching	The student will be able to identify important similarities and differences relative to the information, mental procedure, or psychomotor procedure.
	Classifying	The student will be able to identify superordinate and subordinate categories relative to the information, mental procedure, or psychomotor procedure.
	Analyzing Errors	The student will be able to identify errors in the presentation or use of the information, mental procedure, or psychomotor procedure.
	Generalizing	The student will be able to construct new generalizations or principles based on the information, mental procedure, or psychomotor procedure.
	Specifying	The student will be able to identify logical consequences of the information, mental procedure, or psychomotor procedure.
Level 2: Comprehension	Integrating	The student will be able to identify the basic structure of the information, mental procedure, or psychomotor procedure and the critical as opposed to noncritical characteristics.
	Symbolizing	The student will be able to construct an accurate symbolic representation of the information, mental procedure, or psychomotor procedure differentiating critical and noncritical elements.
Level 1: Retrieval	Recognizing	The student will be able to validate correct statements about features of information, but not necessarily understand the structure of the knowledge or differentiate critical and noncritical components.
	Recalling	The student will be able to produce features of information, but not necessarily understand the structure of the knowledge or differentiate critical and noncritical components.
	Executing	The student will be able to perform a procedure without significant error, but not necessarily understand how and why the procedure works.

Source: Marzano & Kendall (2007)

The rows of Figure 1.3 represent the various levels of the New Taxonomy. The third column of Figure 1.3 portrays a generic form of the objectives that might be generated for each level of the New Taxonomy. Subsequent chapters provide specific examples of educational objectives, along with tasks that might be used to assess those objectives, for each level of the New Taxonomy across the three domains of knowledge. To obtain a sense of the objectives that might be generated and assessed using the New Taxonomy it is useful to start with retrieval objectives—the bottom of the New Taxonomy.

Retrieval objectives involve the recognition, recall, and execution of basic information and procedures. These are very common in education and were addressed in Bloom's "knowledge" level.

Comprehension objectives involve identifying and symbolizing the critical features of knowledge. These too are quite common among educational objectives. *Comprehension* in the New Taxonomy is similar to *comprehension* in Bloom's taxonomy; however, Bloom's taxonomy does not contain a process akin to *symbolizing knowledge*.

Analysis objectives involve reasoned extensions of knowledge. They are sometimes referred to as *higher order* in that they require students to make inferences that go beyond what was directly taught. The New Taxonomy involves five types of analysis processes: matching, classifying, analyzing errors, generating, and specifying. *Matching* in the New Taxonomy is similar to what Bloom refers to as *analysis of relationships* within Level 4.0 (analysis) of his taxonomy. *Classifying* in the New Taxonomy is similar to what Bloom refers to as *identifying a set of abstract relations* within Level 5.0 (synthesis) of his taxonomy. *Analyzing errors* in the New Taxonomy is similar to what is referred to as *judging internal evidence* within Level 6.0 (evaluation) of Bloom's taxonomy. It is also similar to *analysis of organizing principles* within Level 4.0 (analysis) of Bloom's taxonomy. *Generalizing and specifying* in the New Taxonomy are embedded in many components from Levels 4, 5, and 6 of Bloom's taxonomy.

Knowledge utilization objectives are employed when knowledge is used to accomplish a specific task. Such objectives are frequently a part of what some educators refer to as *authentic tasks*. The New Taxonomy includes four knowledge utilization processes: decision making, problem solving, experimenting, and investigating. The overall category of knowledge utilization is most closely related to *synthesis* (Level 5.0) in Bloom's taxonomy.

Metacognitive objectives address setting and monitoring goals. Although the importance of these behaviors is recognized by educators, it is rare that specific objectives are written that involve metacognition. The New Taxonomy includes four types of metacognitive processes: specifying goals, process monitoring, monitoring clarity, and monitoring accuracy. No obvious corollary can be found in Bloom's taxonomy.

Self-system objectives address attitudes, beliefs, and behaviors that control motivation. As is the case with metacognition, self-system processes seem to be valued by educators but are rarely addressed in terms of explicit objectives. The New Taxonomy includes four types of self-system processes: examining importance, examining efficacy, examining emotional response, and examining overall motivation. No obvious corollary can be found in Bloom's taxonomy.

Conclusions

As illustrated in very general terms in Figure 1.3, the New Taxonomy can be used to generate and assess a wide range of objectives covering three domains of knowledge (information, mental procedures, and psychomotor procedures) and three categories of processes (cognitive, metacognitive, and self-system). This is not to say that schools and districts should include objectives for all six levels of the New Taxonomy at all grade levels. As we demonstrate in Chapter 9, we recommend that metacognitive and self-system thinking be considered a complementary and supportive curriculum to the first four levels of the New Taxonomy (retrieval, comprehension, analysis, and knowledge utilization), which are considered more traditionally academic in nature.

CHAPTER TWO

The New Taxonomy in Brief

This chapter briefly describes the various components of the New Taxonomy as a foundation for understanding the discussion in subsequent chapters. We strongly recommend that readers become familiar with the book *The New Taxonomy of Educational Objectives* (Marzano & Kendall, 2007) to obtain a comprehensive understanding of the research and theory supporting the model. Readers who are thoroughly familiar with *The New Taxonomy of Educational Objectives* might wish to skip this chapter.

THE DOMAINS OF KNOWLEDGE DIMENSION

Knowledge can be organized into three broad domains: information, mental procedures, and psychomotor procedures.

The Domain of Information

The domain of information, sometimes referred to as *declarative knowledge*, has a hierarchic structure in its own right. At the bottom of the informational hierarchy are vocabulary terms. A vocabulary term is a word or phrase about which a student has an accurate, but not necessarily deep, level of understanding. For example, a student might have a general understanding of the term *asteroids* but know little of the nuances regarding its defining characteristics and its similarities and differences with comets and meteors. Whether or not a term is considered a vocabulary term within the New Taxonomy is totally a function of instruction. To illustrate, consider the term *habitat*. Obviously it could be the topic of an entire unit of instruction or even more. In this case, habitat would not be considered a vocabulary term. Rather it would be an organizing concept with a variety of related generalization, principles, and facts. In contrast, if treated as a vocabulary term, *habitat* would be addressed very briefly, and the expectation would be that students have a surface level understanding only of some basic characteristic. Instructional focus and intent, then, are major determinants when classifying types of knowledge in the New Taxonomy. This is an important awareness to keep in mind when classifying any type of knowledge— information, mental procedures, or psychomotor procedures—as it relates to the New Taxonomy.

At a level above vocabulary terms are *facts*. Facts present information about specific persons, places, things, and events. To illustrate, "The Battle of Gettysburg was pivotal to the outcome of the Civil War" is a fact. One characteristic of facts is that they commonly involve the definite article *the* with reference to their subject. Instruction again plays a critical role in determining whether specific informational knowledge is considered a fact. To illustrate, consider the statement, "The human skeleton has characteristics similar to and different from the skeleton of a chimpanzee." If the expectation is that students simply know this piece of information without being able to elaborate on specific similarities and differences, then it would be considered a simple fact. However, if the expectation is that students can provide detailed examples of the similarities and differences, then the statement would be considered a generalization. Again, instructional focus and intent are the determiners of the precise classification for a knowledge component.

At the top of the hierarchy are more general structures, such as generalizations and principles. The statement "Specific battles sometimes disproportionately influence the outcome of a war" is a generalization. As mentioned previously, to be considered a generalization, the expectation would be that students can provide detailed examples of this statement.

The various types of knowledge within the information domain are described in more detail in Figure 2.1.

For the sake of clarity and ease of use, the New Taxonomy organizes the types of information into two broad categories: *details* and *organizing ideas*. Details include vocabulary terms, facts, and time sequences; organizing ideas include generalizations and principles.

Details
- Vocabulary terms
- Facts
- Time sequences

Organizing ideas
- Principles
- Generalizations

Figure 2.1   Types of Informational Knowledge

Vocabulary Terms

At the most specific level of informational knowledge are vocabulary terms. In this system, knowing a vocabulary term means understanding the general meaning of a word. For example, when students understand declarative knowledge at the level of a vocabulary term, they have a general idea of what the word means and no serious misconceptions about its meaning. To organize classroom content as vocabulary terms is to organize it as independent words. The expectation is that students have an accurate but somewhat surface-level understanding of the meaning of these terms.

Facts

Facts are a very specific type of informational content. Facts convey information about specific persons, places, living and nonliving things, and events. They commonly articulate information such as the following:

- The characteristics of a specific real or fictitious person (e.g., The fictitious character Robin Hood first appeared in English literature in the early 1800s).
- The characteristics of a specific place (e.g., Denver is in the state of Colorado).
- The characteristics of specific living and nonliving things (e.g., My dog, Tuffy, is a golden retriever; the Empire State Building is over 100 stories high).
- The characteristics of a specific event (e.g., Construction began on the Leaning Tower of Pisa in 1174).

Time Sequences

Time sequences include important events that occurred between two points in time. For example, the events that occurred between President Kennedy's assassination on November 22, 1963, and his burial on November 25, 1963, are organized as a time sequence in most people's memories. First one thing happened, then another, then another.

Generalizations

Generalizations are statements for which examples can be provided. For example, the statement "U.S. presidents often come from families that have great wealth or influence" is a generalization, for which examples can be provided. It is easy to confuse some generalizations with some facts. Facts identify characteristics of *specific* persons, places, living and nonliving things, and events, whereas generalizations identify characteristics about *classes* or *categories* of persons, places, living and nonliving things, and events. For example, the statement "My dog, Tuffy, is a golden retriever" is a fact. However, the statement "Golden retrievers are good hunters" is a generalization. In addition, generalizations identify characteristics about abstractions. Specifically, information about abstractions is typically stated in the form of generalizations. With these distinctions noted, if a generalization (or principle) is treated as an isolated piece of information with no supporting examples or applications, then it should be classified as a fact. Instructional focus and intent are determining factors in the classification of information as generalizations versus facts. The following are examples of the various types of generalizations:

- Characteristics of classes of persons (e.g., It takes at least two years of training to become a fireman.)
- Characteristics of classes of places (e.g., Large cities have high crime rates.)
- Characteristics of classes of living and nonliving things (e.g., Golden retrievers are good hunting dogs; Firearms are the subject of great debate.)
- Characteristics of classes of events (e.g., Super Bowls are premier sporting events in the United States.)
- Characteristics of abstractions (e.g., Love is one of the most powerful human emotions.)

(Continued)

Figure 2.1 (Continued)

Principles

Principles are specific types of generalizations that deal with relationships. In general, there are two types of principles found in school-related declarative knowledge: *cause–effect principles* and *correlational principles.*

Cause–effect principles. These principles articulate causal relationships. For example, the sentence "Tuberculosis is caused by the tubercle bacillus" is a cause–effect principle. Although not stated here, understanding a cause–effect principle includes knowledge of the specific elements within the cause–effect system and the exact relationships those elements have to one another. To understand the cause–effect principle regarding tuberculosis and the bacterium, one would have to understand the sequence of events that occur, the elements involved, and the type and strength of relationships between those elements. In short, understanding a cause–effect principle involves a great deal of information.

Correlational principles. Correlational principles describe relationships that are not necessarily causal in nature but in which a change in one factor is associated with a change in another factor. For example, the following is a correlational principle: "The increase in lung cancer among women is directly proportional to the increase in the number of women who smoke."

Again, to understand this principle, a student would have to know the specific details about this relationship, such as the general pattern, that the number of women who have lung cancer changes at the same rate as the number of women who smoke changes.

These two types of principles are sometimes confused with cause–effect *sequences.* A cause–effect sequence applies to a specific situation, whereas a principle applies to many situations. The causes of the Civil War taken together represent a cause–effect sequence they apply to the Civil War only. However, the cause–effect principle linking tuberculosis and the tubercle bacillus can be applied to many different situations and many different people. Physicians use this principle to make judgments about a variety of situations and a variety of people. The key distinction between principles and cause–effect sequences is that principles can be exemplified in a number of situations, whereas cause–effect sequences cannot—they apply to a single situation only.

Source: Marzano & Kendall (2007)

The Domain of Mental Procedures

Mental procedures—sometimes referred to as *procedural knowledge*—are different in form and function from information or declarative knowledge. Whereas declarative knowledge can be considered the "what" of human knowledge, procedural knowledge can be described as the "how-to." One important characteristic of procedural knowledge is that it contains information. Information is embedded in the domain of mental procedures and the domain of psychomotor procedures.

Procedural knowledge typically starts out as declarative knowledge. To illustrate, consider the procedure for driving a car. In the initial stages, an individual cannot actually drive the car but knows information about driving, such as the location of the brake, the general flow of physical activity needed to turn in different directions, the general flow of activity needed to slow down, speed up, and so on. The individual cannot perform the procedure but is aware of the requirements to do so. With practice over time, the individual learns to execute the procedure, sometimes with little conscious thought. At this point it is fully developed procedural knowledge.

Driving a car is an example of a psychomotor procedure in that it involves physical action. An example of a mental procedure is editing a composition for overall logic. Again, in the initial stages of learning how to edit for overall logic, an individual must know some basic information, such as the characteristics of a logical progression of ideas and the need to reread a composition a number of times to edit effectively. With practice over time, the individual actually learns how to execute the steps involved in editing for overall logic with relative ease.

At the top of the hierarchy of mental procedures are highly robust processes that have a diversity of possible products or outcomes and involve the execution of many interrelated subprocedures. Technically, such operations are referred to as *macroprocedures.* The prefix *macro* indicates that the procedure is highly complex, having many subcomponents that require some form of management. For example, the procedure of writing fulfills the defining characteristics of a macroprocedure.

Somewhat in the middle of the hierarchy are mental procedures that do not generate the variety of products possible from macroprocedures and do not incorporate the wide variety of subcomponents. These procedures are commonly referred to as *tactics.* For example, an individual may have a tactic for reading a histogram. Tactics are made up of general rules with an overall flow of execution. For example, a tactic for reading a histogram might include rules that address (a) identifying the elements depicted in the legend, (b) determining what is reported in each axis on the graph, and (c) determining the relationship between the elements on the two axes. Although there is a general pattern in which these rules are executed, there is no rigid or set order. Again, instructional focus and intent are major determiners in classifying a mental procedure as a macroprocedure versus a tactic. To illustrate, consider the procedure of using a calculator. If approached as a few basic operations, then it would be considered a tactic. However, if approached as a complex set of interacting functions that can be used in a variety of situations, then it would be considered a macroprocedure.

Algorithms are mental procedures that normally do not vary in application once learned. They have very specific outcomes and very specific steps. Multi-column addition and subtraction are illustrations of algorithms. Algorithms must be learned to the level of automaticity to be useful.

The simplest type of mental procedure is a *single rule* or a small set of rules with no accompanying steps. A single rule would consist of one IF–THEN rule— IF situation *X* occurs, THEN perform action *Y.* For example, a rule for capitalizing the first word in a sentence is a single-rule procedure.

For the purpose of the New Taxonomy, it is useful to organize the domain of mental procedures into two broad categories: those that, with practice, can be executed automatically or with little conscious thought and those that must be controlled. Tactics, algorithms, and single rules can be learned to the level of automaticity or to the level of little conscious thought. Macroprocedures require controlled execution. As a set, tactics, algorithms, and single rules will be referred to as *skills* throughout the New Taxonomy; macroprocedures will be referred to simply as *processes*. Again the reader is cautioned that instructional focus and intent play major roles in determining whether a mental procedure is considered a process or a skill. Figure 2.2 depicts the two categories of mental procedures within the New Taxonomy.

Figure 2.2   Categories of Mental Procedures

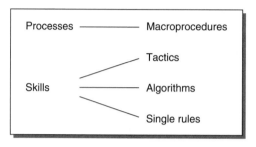

Source: Marzano & Kendall (2007)

The Domain of Psychomotor Procedures

As the name implies, the psychomotor domain is composed of physical procedures. As is the case with the other two domains, the psychomotor domain can be organized into a hierarchy. At the bottom of the psychomotor hierarchy are *foundational physical* abilities upon which more complex procedures are developed. These include overall body equilibrium, speed of limb movement, manual dexterity, and the like.

These foundational abilities are generally developed without formal instruction. Indeed, human beings perform all these physical functions naturally with a certain degree of aplomb. However, this is not to say that these foundational skills cannot be improved with instruction and practice. For example, with instruction, a person's manual dexterity can be improved. Therefore, it qualifies as a type of knowledge in that it can be enhanced through instruction.

At a level up from basic foundational procedures are *simple combination procedures*, such as shooting a free throw in basketball. As their name implies, simple combination procedures involve sets of foundational procedures acting in parallel. Shooting a free throw in basketball is an example of a simple combination procedure that involves the interaction of a number of foundational procedures, such as wrist-finger speed, control precision, and arm-hand steadiness.

Finally, *complex combination procedures* use sets of simple combination procedures. For example, the act of playing defense in basketball involves the combination skills of side-to-side movement with the body in a squatting position, hand waving, and so on. Once again, instructional focus and intent commonly determine if a psychomotor procedure is classified as a simple combination procedure or a complex combination procedure. Consider for example, the procedure of putting together a series of specific movements to create a dance segment. This could be approached in a fairly simplistic manner (i.e., a simple combination procedure) or a complex manner involving sophisticated and highly nuanced transitions (i.e., a complex combination procedure).

For the purposes of the New Taxonomy, it is useful to organize the procedures in the psychomotor domain into two categories. This is illustrated in Figure 2.3.

Figure 2.3   Categories of Psychomotor Procedures

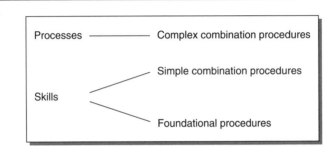

Source: Marzano & Kendall (2007)

In summary, for the purposes of the New Taxonomy, the components in the three domains of knowledge have been organized as depicted in Figure 2.4.

Figure 2.4   Components of the Three Knowledge Domains

Information	1. Organizing ideas	Principles Generalizations
	2. Details	Time sequences Facts Vocabulary terms
Mental Procedures	1. Processes	Macroprocedures
	2. Skills	Tactics Algorithms Single rules
Psychomotor Procedures	1. Processes	Complex combination procedures
	2. Skills	Simple combination procedures Foundational procedures

Source: Marzano & Kendall (2007)

THE LEVELS OF PROCESSING DIMENSION

The second dimension of the New Taxonomy deals with levels of mental processing that are applied to the three knowledge domains. There are three general systems of mental processing that operate in a coordinated fashion: the self-system, the metacognitive system, and the cognitive system. This is depicted in Figure 2.5.

Figure 2.5   Six Levels of the New Taxonomy

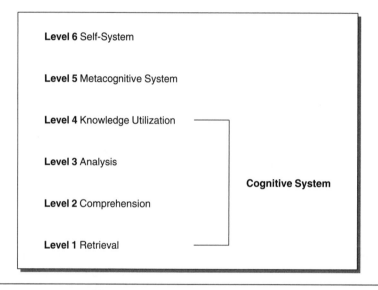

Source: Marzano & Kendall (2007)

As shown in Figure 2.5, the cognitive system includes four subsystems that have a hierarchic structure: retrieval, comprehension, analysis, and knowledge utilization. This makes for a six-level taxonomy.

Level 1: Retrieval (Cognitive System)

Retrieval involves transferring what we know but are currently not thinking about to a current state of attention. The process of retrieval differs somewhat, depending upon the type of knowledge involved and the degree of processing required. In the New Taxonomy, retrieval of **information** is either a matter of *recognition* or *recall*. Recognition can be described as determining whether incoming information is accurate, inaccurate, or unknown. Recall, by contrast, requires not only some level of recognition, but in addition, the production of related information. For example, a student who selects a synonym from among a set of words relies upon recognition. A student asked to define a word or produce a synonym employs recall; in addition to recognizing the term, the student must produce an appropriate response. This distinction constitutes a hierarchy of difficulty within Level 1 of the New Taxonomy.

Although knowledge from the domain of information is only recognized or recalled, knowledge from the domains of **mental procedures** and **psychomotor procedures** can be *executed* as well. When the steps in a procedure are carried out, something occurs, and a product results. For example, consider the procedure for multicolumn subtraction; a quantity is computed when the steps are carried out. Thus we say that procedural knowledge is executed, whereas information is recognized and recalled. However, it is also true that procedural knowledge can be recognized and recalled, because all procedures contain embedded information. (See previous discussion of mental procedures.)

Level 2: Comprehension (Cognitive System)

The process of comprehension within the cognitive system is responsible for identifying the critical or defining attributes of knowledge. Comprehension, as defined in the New Taxonomy, involves two related processes: integrating and symbolizing.

Integrating

Integrating involves distilling knowledge down to its key characteristics organized in a parsimonious, generalized form. Effective learners pare down incoming information to its gist. This explains why individuals usually do not remember the specific facts in an interesting story they have read but do tend to recall the general flow of information and events.

Symbolizing

Symbolizing is the comprehension process of creating a symbolic analog of the knowledge that has been produced via the process of integrating. The symbolic analysis is typically in the form of images. A popular form of symbolizing in K–12 classrooms is graphic organizers, which combine language and symbols. Symbolizing can also take the form of graphs, pictures, and pictographs.

Level 3: Analysis (Cognitive System)

Analysis in the New Taxonomy involves the reasoned extension of knowledge. Analysis also goes beyond the identification of essential versus nonessential characteristics that are a function of the process of comprehension. Analysis in this context involves the generation of new information not already possessed by the individual. There are five analysis processes: (1) matching, (2) classifying, (3) analyzing errors, (4) generalizing and (5) specifying.

Matching

Matching addresses the identification of similarities and differences between knowledge components. The process of matching may be simple or complex, depending on the demands of the task. At a simple level, matching involves noticing basic similarities, like those between two dogs. At a more complex level, matching involves comparing the same two dogs on characteristics that are key features of their respective breeds and explaining *how* these similarities and differences help that breed. It is the latter form of the task that is referred to here as *matching*. Important components of the matching process include

- Specifying the attributes or characteristics on which items being matched are to be analyzed
- Determining how they are alike and different
- Stating similarities and differences as precisely as possible

Classifying

Classifying refers to organizing knowledge into meaningful categories. Like matching, it is basic to human thought. Although learners use the process of classifying naturally, when used as an analytic tool, this process can be very challenging. Classifying is distinct from matching in that it focuses on superordinate and subordinate categories, whereas matching focuses on similarities and differences. Important components of the classifying process include

- Identifying the defining characteristics of the items to be classified
- Identifying a superordinate category to which the item belongs and explaining why it belongs in that category
- Identifying one or more (if any) subordinate categories for the item and explaining how they are related

Analyzing Errors

Analyzing errors addresses the reasonableness, logic, or accuracy of knowledge. The existence of this cognitive function implies that information must be considered reasonable for an individual to accept it as valid. To perform this function well, a student must have a basic (but not necessarily technical) understanding of the nature of evidence and well-formed arguments as well as various types of logical errors one can make. Critical attributes of analyzing informational errors include

- Determining if information as presented appears reasonable
- Analyzing the information for logical errors and inaccuracies

The foregoing discussion applies to error analysis involving information. When the focus is on mental or psychomotor processes, analyzing errors is a quite different matter. Given that procedures commonly involve bugs, analyzing errors for mental and psychomotor procedures involves searching for and remediating bugs. However, the process of analyzing errors must be guided by a conceptual understanding of the procedure. Operationally, this means that students examine the impact of each aspect of a mental or psychomotor procedure from the perspective of its contribution to the overall effectiveness of the procedures. Critical attributes of analyzing errors for procedural knowledge include

- Identifying the impact each step or component of a procedure has on the overall process
- Identifying and correcting a faulty or ineffective step or component

Generalizing

Generalizing, as defined in the New Taxonomy, is the process of constructing new generalizations from information that is already known or observed. To illustrate, a student is involved in the analytic process of generalizing when he or she designs a new generalization about "regions" from three generalizations that have already been presented in class. Critical attributes of generalizing include

- Focusing on specific pieces of information or observations without making assumptions
- Looking for patterns or connections in the information
- Making a general statement that explains the patterns or connections

Specifying

Specifying is the process of generating new applications of a known generalization or principle. To illustrate, a student is involved in the analytic process of specifying by identifying a new situation or new phenomenon that is governed by Bernoulli's principle (which is commonly taught in high school to explain the concept of lift). The student has taken known principles and identified a new application previously not known to the individual.

Critical attributes of specifying include

- Identifying the generalizations or principles that apply to a specific situation
- Making sure that the specific situation meets the conditions that have to be in place for the generalizations or principles to apply
- If the generalizations or principles do apply, identifying what conclusions can be drawn or what predictions can be made

Level 4: Knowledge Utilization (Cognitive System)

As their name implies, knowledge utilization processes are those employed when an individual wishes to accomplish a specific task. For example, an engineer might use the knowledge of Bernoulli's principle to solve a specific problem related to lift in the design of a new type of aircraft. Robust tasks are the venue in which knowledge is rendered useful to individuals. In the New Taxonomy, four general categories of knowledge utilization tasks have been identified: (1) decision making, (2) problem solving, (3) experimenting, and (4) investigating.

Decision Making

The process of decision making is used when an individual must select between two or more alternatives. Decision making might be described as the process by which an individual answers questions like "What is the best way to ____?" or "Which of these is most suitable?" For example, individuals are engaged in decision making when they use their knowledge of specific locations within a city to identify the best site for a new park. Key elements of the decision-making process include

- Identifying alternatives
- Identifying the criteria that will be used to judge the value of each alternative
- Selecting among alternatives based on a systematic application of criteria

Problem Solving

The process of problem solving is used when an individual attempts to accomplish a goal for which an obstacle exists. Problem solving might be described as the process one engages in to answer questions such as "How will I overcome this obstacle?" or "How will I reach my goal but still meet these conditions?" Critical attributes of the problem solving process include

- Identifying obstacles to the goal
- Identifying alternative ways to accomplish the goal
- Evaluating the alternatives
- Selecting and executing the alternatives

Experimenting

Experimenting is the process of generating and testing hypotheses for the purpose of understanding some physical or psychological phenomenon. Experimenting might be described as the process used when answering questions such as "How can this be explained?" or "Based on this explanation, what can be predicted?" For example, an individual is involved in experimental inquiry when he or she generates and tests a hypothesis about the effect a new airplane wing design will have on lift and drag. Critical attributes of experimenting include

- Making predictions based on known or hypothesized principles
- Designing a way to test the predictions using observational data
- Evaluating the validity of the principles based on the outcome of the test

Investigating

Investigating is the process of generating and testing hypotheses about past, present, or future events. Investigating may be described as the process one goes through when attempting to answer such questions as "What are the defining features of_____?" or "How did this happen?" or "Why did this happen?" or "What would have happened if_____?" To illustrate, a student is involved in investigating when he or she examines possible explanations for the existence of the phenomenon known as crop circles by examining what others have said or written on the topic. Critical attributes of investigating include

- Identifying what is known or agreed upon regarding the phenomenon under investigation
- Identifying areas of confusion or controversy regarding the phenomenon
- Providing an answer for the confusion or controversy using opinions and arguments expressed by others
- Presenting a logical argument for the proposed answer

Level 5: Metacognition

The metacognitive system is responsible for monitoring, evaluating, and regulating the functioning of all other types of thought. Taken together, these functions are sometimes referred to as responsible for so-called executive control. Within the New Taxonomy, the metacognitive system has four functions: (1) specifying goals, (2) process monitoring, (3) monitoring clarity, and (4) monitoring accuracy.

Specifying Goals

One of the primary tasks of the metacognitive system is to establish clear goals and plans for accomplishing those goals. In terms of the New Taxonomy, the goal-setting function of the metacognitive system is responsible for establishing clear learning goals for specific types of knowledge. For example, it would be through the goal-specification function of the metacognitive system that a student would establish a specific goal in terms of increasing competence at a specific psychomotor skill taught in a physical education class. Along with the goal, the student would establish a plan for accomplishing the goal.

Process Monitoring

The process-monitoring component of the metacognitive system typically monitors the effectiveness of a procedure as it is being carried out when a specific goal has been identified. For example, the metacognitive system will monitor how well a goal is being met relative to reading a bar graph or how well a goal is being met relative to shooting free throws. Process monitoring also comes into play when a long-term or short-term goal has been established for information, for example, when a student has established the goal of better understanding polynomials.

Monitoring Clarity

Monitoring clarity and monitoring accuracy belong to a set of functions that some researchers refer to as *dispositional*. The term *disposition* is used to indicate that monitoring clarity and monitoring accuracy are ways in which an individual is or is not disposed to approach knowledge. Monitoring clarity involves determining the extent to which an individual is free from indistinction and ambiguity about knowledge.

Monitoring Accuracy

Monitoring accuracy involves determining the extent to which an individual is correct in terms of understanding specific knowledge. It typically requires individuals to check their understanding by seeking out further information.

Level 6: Self-System Thinking

The self-system determines whether an individual will engage in or disengage from a given task; it also determines how much energy the individual will bring to the task. Once the self-system has determined what will be attended to, the functioning of all other elements of thought (i.e., the metacognitive system, the cognitive system, and the knowledge domains) are, to a certain extent, dedicated or determined. There are four types of self-system thinking that are relevant to the New Taxonomy: (1) examining importance, (2) examining efficacy, (3) examining emotional response, and (4) examining overall motivation.

Examining Importance

One of the key determinants of whether an individual attends to a given type of knowledge is whether that individual considers the knowledge important. What an individual considers to be important is probably a function of the extent to which it meets one of two conditions: it is perceived as instrumental in satisfying a basic need, or it is perceived as instrumental in the attainment of a personal goal.

Examining Efficacy

Relative to the New Taxonomy, examining efficacy involves examining the extent to which an individual believes he or she has the ability, power or necessary resources to gain competence relative to a specific knowledge component. If a student believes he or she does not have the requisite ability, power, or resources to gain competence in a specific skill, this might greatly lessen the motivation to learn that knowledge even though it is perceived as important.

Examining Emotional Response

The influence of emotion in human motivation is becoming increasingly clear. Relative to the New Taxonomy, examining emotions involves analyzing the extent to which an individual has an emotional response to a given knowledge component and the part that response plays in one's motivation.

Examining Overall Motivation

As might be inferred from the previous discussion, an individual's motivation to initially learn or increase competence in a given knowledge component is a function of three factors: (1) perceptions of its importance, (2) perceptions of efficacy relative to learning or increasing competency in the knowledge component, and (3) one's emotional response to the knowledge component. This is depicted in Figure 2.6.

Figure 2.6   Aspects of Motivation

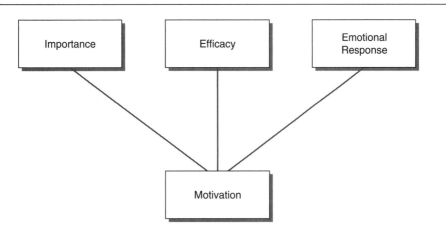

Source: Marzano & Kendall (2007)

Given this set of relationships, one can operationally describe different levels of motivation. Specifically, high motivation to learn or increase competence relative to a given knowledge component will exist under the following conditions:

1. The individual perceives the knowledge component as important, and

2. The individual believes that he or she has the necessary ability, power, or resources to learn or increase competence relative to the knowledge component, or

3. The individual has a positive emotional response to the knowledge component (or both 2 and 3).

Low motivation occurs under the following conditions:

1. The individual perceives the knowledge component to be unimportant, or

2. The individual believes that he or she does not have the necessary ability, power, or resources to learn or increase competence relative to the knowledge component, or

3. The individual has a negative emotional response to the knowledge component.

In terms of the New Taxonomy, examining motivation is the process of identifying one's level of motivation to learn or increase competence in a given knowledge component and then identifying the interrelationships between one's beliefs about importance, beliefs about efficacy, and emotional responses that govern one's level of motivation.

SUMMARY

In summary, the New Taxonomy has a knowledge dimension and a mental processing dimension. Using these two dimensions, educators can design objectives for specific knowledge components involving specific mental processes. Readers not thoroughly familiar with the information presented in this chapter are encouraged to read *The New Taxonomy of Educational Objectives* (Marzano & Kendall, 2007).

Chapters 3 through 8 of this text address each mental-processing level of the New Taxonomy as it relates to each of the three knowledge domains. Chapter 9 addresses the use of the New Taxonomy as a framework for assessment.

CHAPTER THREE

Retrieval Objectives and Tasks

R etrieval involves recognizing, recalling, or executing knowledge. At this level of the New Taxonomy there is no expectation that the student demonstrates the knowledge in depth or understands the basic structure of the knowledge or its critical versus noncritical elements. We consider each of the three types of retrieval.

RECOGNIZING

Recognizing involves determining whether incoming information is accurate, inaccurate, or unknown. Figure 3.1 presents recognizing objectives and tasks for various types of knowledge.

The farthest column to the right of Figure 3.1 (Column 6) contains a prototypical benchmark statement found in many state and district standards documents. The statements in this column demonstrate an important consideration in designing objectives and tasks using state or local standards documents—they can be very generic in their description of their expectations regarding student competence in subject matter content. The examples involve grade-level intervals. When state and district documents write benchmark statements for each grade level, the problem can be alleviated somewhat. However even grade-level benchmark statements can be quite general in nature. To illustrate, here are prototypical statements from state-level standards documents regarding expectations for the English language arts at fifth grade:

1. Apply prior knowledge and experience to make inferences and respond to new information presented in text.

2. Draw inferences and conclusions and support them with textual evidence and prior knowledge.

(*Text continues on page 30*)

Figure 3.1   Recognizing Objectives and Tasks

	Sample Task	Objective	Knowledge Focus	Subject, Grade	Benchmark Statement
Information: Details: Terms, Facts, Time sequences	Which of the following sequences of events and presidential administrations is accurate? a. Kennedy, Berlin Blockade, Truman, Cuban Missile Crisis b. Berlin Blockade, Truman, Kennedy, Cuban Missile Crisis c. Cuban Missile Crisis, Kennedy, Truman, Berlin Blockade d. Truman, Berlin Blockade, Kennedy, Cuban Missile Crisis	The student will be able to identify the correct sequence of critical events at the beginning of the Cold War.	Events at the beginning of the Cold War	History 6–8	Understands how current domestic and international policies have been influenced by the Cold War and conflicts in Korea and Vietnam.
	We have studied the term *consumer price index*. The consumer price index provides an indication of a. Rising stock values b. Inflation c. Supply versus demand d. Retail sales	The student will be able to identify the fact that the consumer price index is an indicator of inflation for consumers.	General characteristics of the term *consumer price index*	Economics 9–12	Knows that the consumer price index shows increases or decreases in price level from one year to another and that inflation is measured by this.
Information: Organizing idea, Generalization	Which of the following is considered a non-renewable resource? a. Timber b. Wind c. Fossil fuel d. Sunlight	The student will be able to identify common renewable and nonrenewable resources from a list.	A generalization regarding the characteristics of renewable and nonrenewable resources	Geography 3–5	Knows the elements of, location of, and use of renewable resources, such as timber, and flow resources, such as wind, as well as nonrenewable resources, such as fossil fuels.

	Sample Task	Objective	Knowledge Focus	Subject, Grade	Benchmark Statement
Information: Organizing idea, Principle	Which of the following could *not* put individuals at higher risk for substance abuse? a. Genetic heritability b. Substance abuse in the family c. Low frustration tolerance d. Birth order	The student will be able to recognize specific conditions that put people at risk for substance abuse.	A principle regarding the relationship between human characteristics and risk for substance abuse	Health 6–8	Knows that substance abuse can be a bigger risk in people with conditions such as genetic inheritance, substance abuse in family or history, and low frustration tolerance.
Mental Procedure: Skill	We have collected data that indicate the proportion of students who prefer one of five types of athletic shoes. What's the *best* way to demonstrate how these preferences appear across all students? a. Pie chart b. Line graph c. List d. Table	The student will be able to identify a pie chart as appropriate for representing proportional data.	The skill of using simple bar and line graphs to represent data	Math 3–5	Creates and understands simple bar and line graphs as well as pie charts.
	Two events are organized on a time line, one after the other. What would *not* be correct to say about them? a. The event on the left side might have caused the event on the right. b. The event on the left side happened earlier than the event on the right side. c. The event on the left side might have been caused by the event on the right.	The student will be able to recognize that interpreting data in a time line relies upon basic assumptions about the possible relationships between past and future events.	The skill of reading a time line	Historical Understanding 3–5	Knows how to identify the time at which events appearing on a time line happened, the sequence in which they occurred, and which other events occurred simultaneously.

(*Continued*)

Figure 3.1 (Continued)

	Sample Task	Objective	Knowledge Focus	Subject, Grade	Benchmark Statement
Mental Procedure: Process	If your class has ten students and three games that just two people can play at one time, how could you find out how many total games must be played so that each student will have a chance to play a game? a. Divide the number of games by the number of players times 2 b. Make a list for each round of games, keeping track of when each student plays c. Use a process of elimination	The student will be able to recognize that using organized lists is an effective problem-solving strategy for systematically accounting for all possibilities.	The general process of problem solving	Math K–2	Organizes lists or tables of Information needed to solve a problem.
	Which of the following would you *not* use in order to determine your level of fitness? __ Cardio-respiratory endurance __ Height __ Muscular strength __ Flexibility	The student will be able to identify from a list what Information is or is not useful when performing a fitness assessment.	The process of performing a fitness assessment	Physical Education 3–6	Improves fitness by interpreting Information from fitness assessments (e.g., cardio-respiratory endurance, muscular strength and endurance, flexibility, and body composition).
Psychomotor Procedure: Skill	Sketching the negative space around an object, rather than drawing the object itself, is done to a. Help improve the perspective of the drawing b. Improve the overall contour of the shape c. Train the eye to see the white space of the drawing d. Make the object appear larger	The student will be able to recognize that sketching negative space helps to train the eye to see the white space of a drawing.	The skill of sketching negative space	Visual Arts 5–8	Knows how experience of and ideas from art media can be enhanced through certain techniques and processes.

	Sample Task	Objective	Knowledge Focus	Subject, Grade	Benchmark Statement
	Which of the following is a defensive play in volleyball? a. spiking the ball b. blocking c. cross-court shot d. decoy	The student will be able to recognize blocking as a defensive play in volleyball.	The skill of blocking in volleyball.	Physical Education 7–8	Identifies sophistication in movement associated with highly skilled physical activities (e.g., moves that distinguish a professional tennis player from a high school tennis player).
Psychomotor Procedure: Process	Which of the following can be useful for projecting a character on stage? — Body alignment — Gestures — Diction — Speaking volume	The student will be able to recognize body alignment, gestures, diction, and speaking volume as useful for projecting a character on stage.	The process of projecting a character using physical techniques	Theatre 5–8	Makes artistic choices by using basic acting skills (e.g., sensory recall, concentration, breath control, diction, body alignment, control of isolated body parts).
	Starting out running somewhat slower than your average speed is a useful strategy in what kind of competition? a. Relay race b. Marathon c. Hurdling d. Sprint	The student will be able to identify starting somewhat slower than average speed as a useful strategy in the marathon.	The process of running a marathon	Physical Education 6–8	Uses basic strategies for both offense and defense in both team and individual sports.

3. Describe elements of character development in written works.

4. Make inferences or draw conclusions about characters' qualities and actions.

5. Participate in creative response to text using art, drama, or oral presentations.

Obviously, to design educational objectives and their related tasks at a specific grade level, educators must frequently "unpack" benchmark statements to cull out specific content on which they will focus.

This unpacking process is depicted in the third and fourth columns of Figure 3.1. Consider the first row of that figure. The benchmark statement reads, "Understands how current domestic policies and international policies have been influenced by the Cold War and conflicts in Korea and Vietnam." The knowledge focus (Column 4) derived from this very general benchmark statement is "Events at the beginning of the Cold War." The recognition objective (Column 3) derived from the knowledge focus is "The student will be able to identify the correct sequence of critical events at the beginning of the Cold War." Where the benchmark statement is quite broad and encompasses the Cold War, Korea, and Vietnam, the objective in this case not only focuses on the Cold War but also calls attention to events at the beginning of the Cold War and their proper sequence.

This example illustrates that objectives derived from a benchmark statement focus on specific elements implied or stated in it and put those elements in a specific context. The fourth column in Figure 3.1 identifies the focus of knowledge that has been culled out of the benchmark statement by a district, school, or individual teacher. Identifying a knowledge focus from benchmark statements is obviously a critical step in designing educational objectives (Column 3) and tasks (Column 2), although it does not have to be done as explicitly as shown in the figure.

Examining the objective statements in Figure 3.1 (see fourth column) illustrates that the verb phrase in some of the objectives is *recognizes*. The various levels of the New Taxonomy represent possible verb phrases that might be used to construct objectives and tasks. As shown in later chapters, at some levels of the New Taxonomy the name of the level does not easily translate into a commonly used verb phrase. In the case of recognizing objectives and tasks, terms and phrases like the following might be used:

- Select from a list
- Identify from a list
- Determine if the following statements are true

In the second column of Figure 3.1, a task is listed for each objective. Tasks represent the behavior students will exhibit as an indication they have met the stated objective. The articulation of specific tasks for each objective provides teachers with explicit guidance as to how they might design assessments. In

Chapter 9 we consider how these tasks can be used to develop a comprehensive system of assessment using the New Taxonomy.

The tasks listed in Figure 3.1 depict the typical formats for recognizing tasks. In general, recognizing tasks are forced-choice in nature. Figure 3.2 lists various types of forced-choice tasks. Any of the formats in Figure 3.2 could have been used with the objectives in Figure 3.1.

It is instructive to consider the nature of recognizing tasks across the various domains of knowledge.

Recognizing With Information

Recognizing tasks for details involve the identification of accurate statements regarding terms, facts, and time sequences. To illustrate, the first task involving details requires students to recognize a correct sequence of events. No in-depth knowledge of these events is required. The second task requires students to identify accurate information about the consumer price index taught at the simple level of a term. Again, no in-depth understanding of the consumer price index is required to complete the task.

Recognizing organizing ideas involves identifying accurate statements about generalizations and principles. To illustrate, the recognizing task for the generalization requires students to identify a simple example of a nonrenewable resource. Again, this does not require in-depth understanding of the defining characteristics of nonrenewable resources and their characteristics.

Recognizing With Mental Procedures

Recognizing tasks for mental skills involve validating accurate statements about a specific mental skill. The first example in Figure 3.1 involves using simple bar graphs and line graphs. Since this procedure is classified as a skill (as opposed to a process), the assumption is that it has been addressed instructionally at a fairly simple level (see Chapter 2 for a discussion). The recognizing task involves identifying the best graph to use in a specific situation. Recognizing tasks for mental processes involve validating accurate statements about a specific mental process. The first mental process in Figure 3.1 is problem solving. Because it is classified as a process (as opposed to a skill), the assumption is that it has been addressed instructionally at a fairly complex level (for a discussion see Chapter 2). The recognizing task requires students to identify components of the problem-solving process from a list.

Recognizing With Psychomotor Procedures

Recognizing tasks for psychomotor skills involve validating accurate statements about a specific mental skill. The first psychomotor *skill* in Figure 3.1 is

Figure 3.2   Types of Forced-Choice Items

1. **Traditional Multiple Choice**—Provides a stem and alternatives, some of which are distracters and one of which is the correct choice
   (Stem) The best definition of a region is. . . .
   A. An area of land between two bodies of water (distracter)
   B. An area of land that has common topographical or political features (correct choice)
   C. An area of land that is a specific size (distracter)
   D. An area of land that has a specific shape (distracter)

2. **Matching**—Provides multiple stems and multiple options
   Traditional format

Invention		Inventor
_____ 1. Vaccine for Polio		A. Eli Whitney
		B. Jonas Salk
_____ 2. Telephone		C. Henry Ford
		D. Alexander Graham Bell
_____ 3. Assembly Line		E. Henry McCormick

   Expanded format

Person	Activity	Time
A. Kennedy	1. Led U.S. forces in Europe (WWII)	6. About 1790
B. Jefferson	2. Elected first Roman Catholic president	7. About 1980
C. Reagan	3. Elected first president of U.S.	8. About 1800
	4. Purchased Louisiana Territory	9. About 1860
	5. Hostages released at start of presidency	10. About 1960

3. **Alternative Choice**—Provides a stem and two choices that are quite similar
   Traditional format
   (Stem) The part of speech used to form a clause is . . .
   A. A preposition
   B. A conjunction

   Alternative format
   (A. An architect, B. A draftsman) is an engineer who designs buildings.

3. **True–False**—Provides statements that must be judged as true or false
   Mark F is the statement is false and T if the statement is true:
   _____ 1. The first thing to do with an automobile that does not start is to check the battery.
   _____ 2. A cause of premature tire wear is improper tire pressure.
   _____ 3. The automobile's onboard computer should be replaced if it drives poorly.
   _____ 4. Under harsh driving conditions, an automobile's oil should be changed every three months or 3,000 miles, whichever comes first.

4. **Multiple Response**—Allows for two or more correct responses.
   Traditional format
   Which of the following can be the end punctuation for a sentence?
   1. A period
   2. A dash
   3. An exclamation point
   4. A question mark
   5. 1 and 2
   6. 2, 3, and 4
   7. 1, 3, and 4
   8. 2 and 3

   Alternative format
   Place a Y in front of each event listed below that occurred at the Battle of Gettysburg:
   _____ 1. Pickett's Charge
   _____ 2. The end of the Civil War
   _____ 3. Confederate soldiers occupied Culp's Hill
   _____ 4. Meade's Maneuver
   _____ 5. Fifteen citizens of Gettysburg were killed at Devil's Den

Source: Adapted from *Classroom Assessment and Grading that Work* (Figure 4.7, p 77). Marzano, Robert J. Alexandria, VA: ASCD, 2006.

sketching negative space. The recognizing task involves identifying the correct reason for sketching negative space among a list of options. Recognizing tasks for psychomotor processes involve validating accurate statements about a specific mental process. The first psychomotor *process* in Figure 3.1 is projecting a character on stage. The task requires identification of appropriate physical techniques within the overall process of projecting a character on stage.

RECALLING

Recalling involves producing accurate information as opposed to simply recognizing it. Figure 3.3 presents recalling objectives and tasks for various types of knowledge.

As before, the benchmark statements in Figure 3.3 are very general. Consequently, a knowledge focus has been identified in the fourth column from which objectives and tasks are designed. Some objectives and tasks employ the verb *recall*. However, other terms like the following might also be used:

- Exemplify
- Name
- List
- Label
- State
- Describe
- Who
- What
- Where
- When

Generally, the format for recalling tasks is short written or oral constructed-response formats as illustrated in Figure 3.3. However, on occasion, fill-in-the-blank formats like the following are used:

As it relates to the cell membrane, the term *selectively permeable* means that the membrane _____.

Recalling With Information

Recalling tasks for details involve producing accurate but not necessarily critical information about terms, facts, and time sequences. The first example of a recalling task for *details* involves factual information regarding the U.S. Constitution. To complete the recalling task, students must retrieve from their permanent memories one way that the U.S. Constitution limits the power of government. The first example of a recalling task for an *organizing idea* addresses a generalization about the impact of chance events on history. The task requires

Figure 3.3 Recalling Objectives and Tasks

	Task	Objective	Knowledge Focus	Subject, Grade	Benchmark Statement
Information: Details: Terms, Facts, Time sequences	Name one way by which the U.S. Constitution limits the powers of government.	The student will be able to name at least one way in which the U.S. Constitution limits the powers of government, such as by separation and sharing of powers, checks and balances, or the Bill of Rights.	Facts about U.S. Constitution	History 6–8	Understands how elements in the U.S Constitution, such as separation and sharing of powers, checks and balances, and the Bill of Rights, serve to limit governmental power.
	What was necessary before the results of early studies linking smoking and cancer were accepted as accurate?	The student will be able to recall that early studies on the link between smoking and cancer were repeated and yielded consistent results before they were accepted as accurate.	Facts about early studies linking smoking and cancer	Science 6–8	Knows that before the results of an experiment are considered valid, they must be found repeatedly and consistently.
Information: Organizing Generalization	In history, we have chance events that are unexpected but can greatly influence events. Identify an example of a chance event that had a significant impact on the events that followed.	The student will be able to identify that a chance event in history is an event that was not planned or anticipated by the participants and can recall one such event from recent readings in history.	A generalization about characteristics of chance events	History 5–6	Understands that chance plays a role in historical events.

	Task	Objective	Knowledge Focus	Subject, Grade	Benchmark Statement
Information: Organizing Principle	We have been studying the law that whenever an object is seen to speed up or slow down, an unbalanced force acts on it. What are some examples of unbalanced forces we see in everyday life? Describe the impact that these forces have.	The student will be able to provide everyday examples that demonstrate the law of unbalanced forces.	A principle regarding unbalanced forces and the speed of objects	Science 6–8	Knows that whenever an object visibly speeds up, slows down, or changes direction, an unbalanced force (e.g., friction) has acted upon it.
Mental Procedure: Skill	What is an example of a situation in which knowing an effective refusal skill is useful?	The student will be able to remember the types of circumstances in which refusal skills are useful.	Refusal skills	Health 9–12	Knows how bad situations can be avoided by using skills such as refusal, negotiation, and collaboration.
	Why would you want to calculate your heart rate and breathing rate when exercising?	The student will be able to recall that heart and breathing rate are components of a fitness assessment.	Calculating heart rate and breathing rate	Physical Education 3–6	Enhances fitness through use of assessment techniques (e.g., cardio-respiratory endurance, muscular strength and endurance, flexibility, and body composition).
Mental Procedure: Process	If you were doing research on a recent event and considering whether a specific book might be useful, why might you check the publication date, the table of contents, and read the preface?	The student will be able to recall that useful Information can be provided by a book's publication date, table of contents, and preface.	Using a book to obtain Information	Language Arts 3–5	Uses the index, table of contents, glossary, appendix, and preface correctly to locate Information.

(Continued)

Figure 3.3 (Continued)

	Task	Objective	Knowledge Focus	Subject, Grade	Benchmark Statement
	Describe why estimation can be useful as part of solving a problem and after you have solved a problem.	The student will be able to describe the value of estimation in solving some problems and for checking the reasonableness of computational results.	Estimating strategies	Math 3–5	Estimates and evaluates estimations through use of strategies such as front-end estimation and rounding.
Psychomotor Procedure: Skill	Why is it important to place your fingers on the home row before you begin typing?	The student will be able to identify the importance of the home row for correct fingering.	Specific keyboarding techniques	Technology K–2	Uses correct hand positions and body posture when typing on a computer keyboard.
	What is the proper way to execute a sit-up?	The student will be able to recall that the knees should be bent during a sit-up.	Doing sit-ups	Physical Education 3–6	Engages in activities such as push-ups, pull-ups, sit-ups, and isometric strength activities in order to develop and maintain muscular strength.
Psychomotor Procedure: Process	There are common individual and team strategies for keeping the ball or puck away from opponents in invasion games, like basketball and hockey. List two or more of these strategies.	The student will be able to list the strategies that are common to individuals and teams for keeping the ball or puck away from opponents.	Playing net and invasion games	Physical Education 3–6	Uses beginning strategies for net and invasion games (e.g., striking a ball to keep it up or away from opponent in a racket sport or dribbling to prevent an opponent from stealing the ball in basketball).
	Why is it important to keep your left hand well under the neck when playing the guitar?	The student will be able to recall that hand position is one of the most important aspects of playing the guitar.	Playing a musical instrument	Music 3–5	Performs with attention to pitch, rhythm, physical dynamics, and timbre when playing a musical instrument.

students to produce examples of how chance events affect history. Again, in-depth knowledge is not required.

Recalling With Mental Procedures

Recalling tasks for mental *skills* involve generating basic information about a mental skill. The first recalling task for a mental skill involves refusal skills. Students must provide an example of when refusal skills might be useful. Recalling tasks for mental *processes* involve producing accurate information about a specific mental process. The first recalling task for a mental process involves the process of using a book to obtain information. Students must retrieve information about how to use the publication date, table of contents, and a preface when obtaining information from a book.

Recalling With Psychomotor Procedures

Recalling tasks for psychomotor skills involve generating information about a specific psychomotor skill. The first recalling task for a psychomotor *skill* involves specific keyboarding techniques. Students must produce information about the importance of the home row. Recalling tasks for psychomotor *processes* involve producing information about a specific psychomotor process. The first recalling task for a psychomotor process involves net and invasion games. Students must produce information about strategies used in various games of this type.

EXECUTING

Executing involves actually carrying out a mental or physical procedure as opposed to simply retrieving or recalling information about such procedures. There is a great deal of misunderstanding regarding the process of executing, particularly as it relates to complex mental and psychomotor procedures. While it is true that executing is at the lowest level of the New Taxonomy (retrieval), it can be the highest level of expectation for students when a complex mental or psychomotor procedure is involved. Consider, for example, the mental process of writing a persuasive essay. The actual execution of this process is a complex feat, indeed, requiring the management of many interacting components. The same can be said for the process of playing basketball, a psychomotor procedure. How, then, could a district, school, or teacher ever expect students to use higher levels of the New Taxonomy, such as articulating critical versus noncritical components of these procedures (i.e., an integrating task) or creating new generalizations about these procedures (i.e., a generalization task), or investigating the origins of these procedures (an investigation task) and so on? The answer is that executing, in fact, might be the highest level of expectation for students for these complex procedures. Stated differently, a district, school, or teacher might not have objectives above the executing level in the New Taxonomy for complex procedures like writing a persuasive essay and playing basketball.

Another option is to break these complex procedures into smaller component parts. Recall from the discussion in Chapter 2 that procedures like these are technically referred to as *macroprocedures* with many subcomponents interacting in complex ways. At a specific grade level, a school or district might focus on one or two elements only for a complex procedure. For example, at lower grade levels, the skill of stating a clear claim might be the emphasis for the complex procedure of writing a persuasive essay. Likewise, at lower grade levels, the emphasis might be placed on dribbling only as it relates to the complex procedure of playing basketball. With these more narrow foci, districts and schools can then legitimately include objectives for the other levels of the New Taxonomy without the fear of overwhelming students. Marzano and Haystead (2008) have outlined how districts and schools might accomplish this spiraling effect to curriculum in the areas of language arts, mathematics, science, and social studies.

Figure 3.4 presents executing objectives and tasks for various types of knowledge.

Theoretically, all of the objective statements in Figure 3.4 could have employed the term *execute,* but none do. This is because the term, although accurate, is simply not common within discussions of procedural knowledge. For example, it would be considered clumsy to say, "The student will be able to execute the skill of determining the next number in a numeric series." Instead, the verbs in executing objectives and tasks are usually specific to the type of skill or process that is the target of the objective or task, like the following:

- Add
- Subtract
- Multiply
- Divide
- Apply
- Demonstrate
- Draft
- Complete
- Locate
- Make
- Solve
- Read
- Use
- Write

Figure 3.4 Executing Objectives and Tasks

	Task	Objective	Knowledge Focus	Grade/Subj.	Benchmark Statement
Information: Details: Terms, Facts, Time sequences	n/a				
	n/a				
Information: Organizing Generalization	n/a				
Information: Organizing Principle	n/a				
Mental Procedure: Skill	Determine your current heart and breathing rate.	The student will be able to monitor heart and breathing rates.	Monitoring heart rate and breathing rate	Physical Education 3–6	Knows how to monitor elements such as heart rate, breathing rate, perceived exertion, and recovery rate in order to determine intensity of exercise.
	Provide the next number in this series: 7, 11, 14, 18, 21, ___.	The student will be able to discover and execute the rule for a specific numeric pattern.	Determining the rule for a pattern of numbers	Math 3–5	Recognizes a wide variety of patterns, such as basic linear patterns, simple repeating and growing patterns and their governing rules.
Mental Procedure: Process	Write a persuasive essay with special attention to the interests and perspectives of an audience of your choice.	The student will be able to write a persuasive essay that reflects attention to the interests and perspectives of a specific audience.	Writing a persuasive essay	Language Arts 3–5	Writes for different audiences, such as self, peers, teachers, and adults, by using strategies such as focus adaptation, organization, point of view, and audience awareness.

(Continued)

Figure 3.4 (Continued)

	Task	Objective	Knowledge Focus	Grade/Subj.	Benchmark Statement
	If the earth's diameter is 12,740 km, what is its circumference? Show how you solved this problem.	The student will be able to solve a variety of problems involving perimeter.	Solving a variety of problems involving perimeter	Math 6–8	Solves perimeter and area problems for a variety of shapes (e.g., parallelograms, triangles, circles).
Psychomotor Procedure: Skill	Tap out the rhythm of ¾, or waltz, time.	The student will be able to initiate and keep a specified rhythm.	Keeping rhythm	Music 3–5	Performs with awareness of pitch, rhythm, dynamics and timbre, and tempo.
	Type the paragraph given you, starting with your fingers on the home row and using appropriate fingering.	The student will be able to type using appropriate fingering.	Using appropriate fingering while typing	Technology 3–5	Performs from home row with awareness of proper fingering and proper posture.
Psychomotor Procedure: Process	Swim two laps, moving from back stroke, to side stroke, to breast stroke in any order, making smooth transitions from one to the other.	The student will be able to demonstrate advanced swimming strokes.	Using various swimming strokes	Physical Education 9–12	Uses advanced sport-specific technique in a variety of activities (e.g., swimming, dance, kayaking, individual and team sports).
	Perform a musical composition of your choice. Pay attention to your tempo and other dynamics we have studied.	The student will be able to perform a musical composition on pitch, in rhythm, with appropriate dynamics and timbre and a steady tempo.	Performing a musical composition	Music 3–5	Performs with awareness of pitch, rhythm, dynamics and timbre, and tempo.

The format for the tasks in Figure 3.4 are short written or oral constructed-response formats accompanied by actually performing (i.e., executing) the procedure. In the case of mental skills, forced-choice formats could have been used. To illustrate, the format for the mental procedure regarding numeric series could have been a multiple-choice task like the following:

Which of the following is the next number you would expect in the series, 7, 11, 14, 18, 21?

    a. 20

    b. 21

    c. 22

    d. 24

Executing With Information

By definition, *executing* does not apply to the domain of information. Information can be recognized and recalled but not executed.

Executing With Mental Procedures

Executing tasks for mental skills involves accurately carrying out the mental skill or process without significant error but not necessarily being able to explain how it works. The first example of an executing task for a mental skill involves monitoring heart rate and breathing rate. For this task students must actually carry out the procedure as opposed to providing information about the procedure. The first example of an executing task for a mental process involves writing a persuasive essay. To complete this task, students must actually write a persuasive essay. Again, it is important to remember that executing can be the highest level of expectation for mental processes.

Executing With Psychomotor Procedures

Executing tasks for psychomotor skills involve accurately carrying out a psychomotor skill or process without significant error but not necessarily being able to explain how it works. The first example of an executing task for a psychomotor skill involves tapping out rhythm. To demonstrate competence in this skill, students must perform the task. The first example of an execution task for a psychomotor process involves using specific strokes while swimming. Students must execute these strokes in a coordinated fashion. Again, executing can be the highest level of expectation for psychomotor processes.

SUMMARY OF KEY POINTS FOR
RETRIEVAL OBJECTIVES AND TASKS

Recognizing Objectives and Tasks

- Require students to validate the accuracy of information presented to them
- Use terms and phrases like the following: recognize, select from a list, identify from a list, determine if the following statements are true
- Use forced-choice formats

Recalling Objectives and Tasks

- Require students to produce accurate information
- Use terms like the following: recall, exemplify, name, list, label, state, describe, who, what, where, when
- Use short written and oral constructed-response formats along with fill-in-the-blank formats

Executing Objectives and Tasks

- Do not apply to the domain of information
- Require students to carry out a procedure
- Can be the highest level of expectation for complex processes
- Use terms like the following: add, subtract, multiply, divide, apply, demonstrate, draft, complete, make, solve, read, use, write
- Use short written and oral constructed-response formats along with execution of the procedure; use forced-choice formats with mental skills

CHAPTER FOUR

Comprehension Objectives and Tasks

Comprehension involves the related processes of integrating and symbolizing knowledge. Critical to both of these processes is that students are able to identify the critical or essential information as opposed to the noncritical or nonessential information.

INTEGRATING

Integrating involves identifying and articulating the critical or essential elements of knowledge. Figure 4.1 presents integrating objectives and tasks for the various types of knowledge.

Benchmark statements sometimes make direct allusion to integrating, at least for the domain of information. For example, consider the benchmark statement in the first row, which states that students are expected to understand the decline of the Cold War from the 1970s to the early 1990s. Implicit in this statement is the expectation that students will distinguish between critical versus noncritical events.

The verb *integrate* is rarely if ever used with integrating objects and tasks. Rather, terms and phrases like the following are frequently employed:

- Describe how or why (or both)
- Describe the key parts of
- Describe the effects
- Describe the relationship between
- Explain ways in which
- Make connections between
- Paraphrase
- Summarize

Figure 4.1   Integrating Objectives and Tasks

	Task	Objective	Knowledge Focus	Grade/Subj.	Benchmark Statement
Information: Details: Terms, Facts, Time sequences	What events external to the Soviet Union were critical to its collapse? Which internal pressures toward collapse were not affected by these events?	The student will be able to identify important external events that led to the collapse of the Soviet Union as opposed to those causes that were solely internal.	Key external events that led to the collapse of the Soviet Union.	World History 7–8	Understands the decline of the Cold War from the 1970s to the early 1990s.
	What recent actions of our federal government have contributed to a market economy?	The student will be able to describe which of the current actions of the United States government have contributed to the market economy.	Recent actions of the United States government that contribute to a market economy.	Economics 6–8	Knows that a market economy operates by the government helping markets operate by protecting property rights (i.e., the right to exclude others from using a good or service and the right to transfer ownership), by providing a system of weights and measures as well as a standard and stable currency.
Information: Organizing Generalization	It is often said that all politics is local; that ultimately individuals respond to their immediate political environment rather than from a national perspective. Identify an election or controversy we have studied in which this generalization has proved to be true. Explain why your example illustrates the critical aspects of this generalization.	The student will be able to provide, by way of example and explanation, evidence of the generalization that individuals tend to respond to and participate in the political process from a local rather than a national perspective.	A generalization about involvement in the political process.	Civics 9–12	Knows that political participation can range from engaging (voting) at the local, state, and national levels to influencing public policy through attending political meetings and demonstrations as well as contacting public or concerned officials through use of letter writing, petitioning, or boycotting.

	Task	Objective	Knowledge Focus	Grade/Subj.	Benchmark Statement
Information: Organizing Principle	A basic principle about the weather concerns how the sun's heat creates weather on earth. Describe how the tilt of the earth and its revolution around the sun affects the seasons.	The student will be able to provide a description showing how the tilt and revolution of the earth around the sun affects the seasons.	A principle regarding the season and the tilt of the earth.	Science 6–8	Knows how seasons and weather patterns of the earth are designed and altered by the tilt of the earth's axis and the earth's revolution around the sun (i.e., heat is more intense on one part or another of the earth according to its revolution around the sun).
Mental Procedure: Skill	Describe the reasoning for the steps used in subtracting fractions with unlike denominators.	The student will identify why each step in adding or subtracting fractions with unlike denominators is important.	The skill of subtracting fractions with unlike denominators.	Math 6–8	Performs addition and subtraction for fractions with unlike denominators and multiples and divides all fractions.
	What problem in sentence meaning is created by a "dangling participle"? What logical steps lead to its correction?	The student will be able to identify the logical problem presented by a dangling participle and how it can be corrected.	The skill of recognizing and correcting dangling modifiers.	Language Arts 6–8	Uses different verb forms in writing (e.g., linking and auxiliary verbs, verb phrases, and regular and irregular verbs).
Mental Procedure: Process	If you wanted to conduct a survey a sample of students to estimate the percentage of students in your class that are informed about a current event, describe how you would choose the survey respondents. Explain why each step in the process is important.	The student will be able to describe the key steps involved in selecting a sample.	The process of sampling within a survey study.	Science 6–8	Uses tools such as computer hardware and software to gather, analyze, and interpret scientific data.

(Continued)

Figure 4.1 (Continued)

	Task	Objective	Knowledge Focus	Grade/Subj.	Benchmark Statement
	What are the most important things to keep in mind when constructing a well-formed paragraph that effectively works within a larger essay or composition? Explain why the steps you have identified are important.	The student will be able to explain how to construct a well-structured paragraph and how it serves the overall purpose of the composition.	The process of writing well-formed paragraphs.	Language Arts 3–5	Uses strategies to edit, draft, and revise writing (e.g., writes with attention to word choice and sentence variation as well as audience; uses paragraphs properly; elaborates on a central idea; produces multiple drafts).
Psychomotor Procedure: Skill	Describe the typical fingering used for a playing a scale on a specific musical instrument. Also explain why this fingering is important.	The student will be able to identify why the fingering for a specific musical instrument is important for playing scales.	The skill of fingering while playing a scale on a specific instrument.	Music 3–5	Uses rhythmic, melodic, and harmonic classroom instruments (e.g. piano, violin, electric guitar, drums) to perform simple chordal patterns accurately and independently.
	Describe how to hold a pencil so that it is easier to form letters clearly. Why does holding a pencil this way help you write better?	The student will be able to explain how to hold a pencil while writing.	The skill of holding a pencil correctly when writing.	Language Arts PreK	Enhances writing with use of tools and materials such as crayons, markers, poster board, and chalkboard.
Psychomotor Procedure: Process	In class we have been learning how to play softball. Describe what you would do during a game if you were the pitcher on the team.	The student will be able to explain how to play softball.	The general process involved in playing softball.	Physical Education 3–5	Understands the general process of playing a major sport.
	Describe how you would go about applying colors and forms in a landscape paying particular attention to the type of brushstrokes you would use during each phase of the process. Defend why the steps you have identified are important.	The student will be able to explain the nuances of applying colors and forms in landscape painting while using a specific set of brush strokes.	The process of applying colors while using a specific set of brush strokes.	Visual Arts 9–12	Understands how the communication of ideas is affected by the techniques and processes used and how this relates to the media.

The most common format for integrating tasks is an extended written or oral constructed response. For example, except for those involving details, all of the tasks in Figure 4.1 would require a fair amount of explanation.

Integrating With Information

In some situations, integrating can be applied to details; however, since integrating involves identifying essential versus nonessential elements, a set of details must have a fairly complex structure to be amenable to integrating. For example, the first integrating task involves details about the key external events that led to the collapse of the Soviet Union. There are a number of such events, and these events have a fairly complex relationship. To complete the task, students have to list the critical events from the set. Given their inherent complexity, organizing ideas are highly amenable to integrating. When generalizations are the focus of integrating, the task involves identifying the defining characteristics of a class of elements. For example, the integrating task involving a generalization addresses a generalization about participation in the political process. The student must provide an example of this generalization and explain how the example meets the defining characteristics of the generalization. Principles are different from generalizations. Principles involve a statement about the relationship between two variables. Consequently, integrating tasks for principles require students to explain the functional relationship between variables. For example, the integrating task involving a principle about the relationship between the tilt of the earth and the seasons requires students to articulate the causal relationship between these two phenomena.

Integrating With Mental Procedures

Integrating tasks for mental skills and processes involve identifying and articulating the important steps of specific skills or processes. The first integrating task involving a mental skill addresses subtracting fractions with like denominators. Students must describe the reasoning underlying the steps in this procedure. The first integrating task for mental processes involves the procedure for sampling within a survey study. Again students must describe the process. Again it is worth noting that with complex procedures—mental and psychomotor—educational objectives are rarely written beyond the level of execution. The typical expectation is that students perform the procedures with fluency and accuracy, not that they can explain the logic of the procedures. Integration goes beyond the typical expectation of executing a procedure and requires understanding the logic underlying the procedure.

Integrating With Psychomotor Procedures

Integrating applies to psychomotor skills and processes the same way it applies to mental skills and processes. A student must identify the steps involved in the skill or process and the logic underlying those steps. The first integrating task for psychomotor skills involves fingering for a specific musical instrument while playing scales. The student must describe the steps involved in this procedure and the logic behind these steps. The first integrating task for psychomotor processes involves the process of playing softball. Students must explain the overall events in this psychomotor process.

It is important to make a distinction between *recalling* as it relates to procedures and *integrating* as it relates to procedures. With recalling, students must simply retrieve the steps involved in a procedure. With integrating, students must explain the logic behind those steps—why they work.

SYMBOLIZING

Symbolizing involves depicting the critical aspects of knowledge in some type of nonlinguistic or abstract form. Figure 4.2 presents symbolizing tasks for the various types of knowledge.

The process of symbolizing is rarely explicit in benchmark statements. That is, benchmark statements rarely ask students to represent or depict knowledge. The term *symbolize* is frequently used in symbolizing objectives and tasks. Other terms and phrases include

- Depict
- Represent
- Illustrate
- Draw
- Show
- Use models
- Diagram
- Chart

The obvious format for symbolizing tasks is a representation that does not rely on language. However, this does not mean that language is incompatible with symbolizing tasks. Indeed, extended explanations and presentations in constructed-response formats often accompany symbolizing tasks. For example, almost every symbolizing task in Figure 4.2 requires students to use language to one extent or another. In many situations some type of graphic organizer is employed. These are somewhat different for the various domains of knowledge.

Symbolizing With Information

Symbolizing as it relates to details can be done in a variety of ways, including pictures, pictographs and graphic organizers. When graphic organizers are employed, the formats found in Figure 4.3 are commonly employed.

Figure 4.2   Symbolizing Objectives and Tasks

	Task	Objective	Knowledge Focus	Grade/Subj.	Benchmark Statement
Information: Details: Terms, Facts, Time sequences	In this unit, we have discussed the waves of immigrants coming to the United States after the Civil War. On a world map outline, draw lines extending from the immigrants' countries of origin to the points in the United States that they most commonly settled. Use wider lines or bands to indicate what countries were the source of a larger numbers of immigrants.	The student will be able to graphically represent immigration after the Civil war in terms of the immigrants' countries of origin as well as relative numbers.	Details of immigration to the United States after the Civil War	History 5–6	Knows about factors that led to increased immigration in the United States during the antebellum period from China, Ireland, and Germany and the ways immigrants adjusted to life in the United States. Knows about the reaction to immigrants from the nativist movement and the "Know-Nothing" party.
	Use a graphic to indicate the arc of the three-act play we have just studied, indicating the key events and characters' actions that move the play forward, including climax and resolution of the play.	The student will be able to illustrate the arc of a three-act play, identifying the key events and character actions, including climax and resolution of the play.	Details of a specific play	Language Arts 6–8	Knows how a plot develops (e.g., parallel story lines and subplots, cause-and-effect relationships, climax, and resolution).
Information: Organizing Generalization	There is a saying that the more things change, the more they stay the same, meaning that although some things might look very different in one way, in other ways they have not changed at all. For example, children used to go to one-room schoolhouses, with every grade in the same room. Once they were inside though, they learned the same spelling and arithmetic you do. If you were to draw this, you might show all the things that were different about the schoolhouses,	The student will be able to illustrate the idea that there are commonalities as well as differences between the present day and the past.	A generalization about the commonalities between the past and the present	History K–4	Understands how families interacted in the past (e.g., roles, jobs, schooling experiences) and how those interactions have changed through time.

(Continued)

Figure 4.2 (Continued)

	Task	Objective	Knowledge Focus	Grade/Subj.	Benchmark Statement
	but also show the same lessons being taught in both places. Think about other ways that life today is similar to and different from life long ago. Draw pictures to illustrate how things have changed and how they have stayed the same.				
Information: Organizing Principle	Illustrate the relationship between supply and demand and their impact on price.	The student will be able to graphically illustrate the relationship between supply and demand.	A principle about the relationship between supply and demand	Economics 3–5	Understands that sellers want to sell more of a product when the prices are higher and buyers want to buy more of a product when the prices are lower.
Mental Procedure: Skill	Represent how you might read the following newspaper article.	The student will be able to visually represent a logical approach to reading a newspaper article.	The skill of reading a simple newspaper article	Language Arts 3–5	Uses text headings, topic and summary sentences, graphic features, typeface, and chapter titles) to find information and main idea.
Mental Procedure: Process	Imagine you have to explain to a younger student why two-fifths plus three-fifths equal one. Use drawings to explain the idea.	The student will be able to illustrate the process of adding simple fractions.	The skill of adding simple fractions	Math 3–5	Uses addition and subtraction for simple fractions.
	Using the provided word problem, translate the problem into variables and symbols for appropriate operations.	The student will be able to use variables to represent a word problem.	The process of solving word problems	Math 6–8	Knows that equations and inequalities are mathematical statements using numbers and symbols to represent relationships and real-world situations.

	Task	Objective	Knowledge Focus	Grade/Subj.	Benchmark Statement
	Use your own notation system to represent the process you use when exploring a new web site. Use different clusters to represent what you do when you are seeking specific information, when you want to check the authenticity of the site, and when you want to understand the different kinds of material that are available from a site.	The student will be able to represent the flow of an information search that uses text features and hierarchic structures in web-based informational text.	The process of using web-based information searches	Language Arts 9–12	Understands complex, implicit hierarchic structures in informational texts, including Internet databases.
Psychomotor Procedure: Skill	Illustrate the required alignment of the tip of the cue stick to the cue ball in order to draw the cue ball back and to the right after it impacts with the object ball.	The student will be able to identify the point of cue stick impact on the cue ball and the subsequent ball trajectory for a given billiard problem.	The skill of striking a billiard ball	Physical Education 7–8	Understands key elements of advanced movement in sports.
	Illustrate the proper arm and hand motion in a butterfly stroke.	The student will be able to illustrate the proper arm and hand motion for the butterfly stroke.	The arm and hand motion for a butterfly stroke	Physical Education 7–8	Understands key elements of advanced movement in sports.
Psychomotor Procedure: Process	Use an S graph to indicate dynamics of a ski turn. Indicate the changing pressure on the uphill and downhill ski and the orientation of the skis and the skier's torso to the fall line.	The student will be able to illustrate an S turn, indicating the position of the skier's torso and skis relative to the fall line, as well as the changing pressure on the uphill and downhill skis throughout the turn.	The process of making an S turn in skiing	Physical Education 7–8	Understands movements associated with highly skilled physical athletes (e.g., moves that lead to successful navigation of a slope while downhill skiing).
	Use an illustration to indicate how to parallel park on a busy street and then return to the flow of traffic.	The student will be able to illustrate the overall process of parallel parking.	The process of parallel parking	Driver's Education 9–12	Demonstrates critical aspects of driving in an urban environment.

Figure 4.3   Graphic Organizers for Details

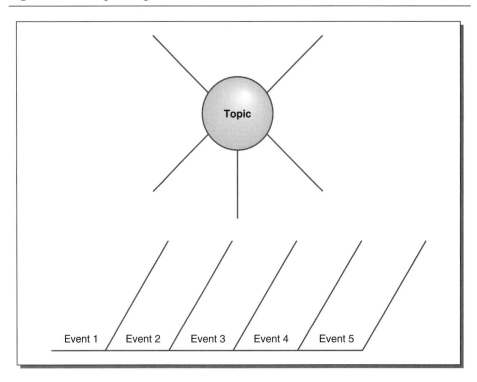

The graphic organizer at the top of Figure 4.3 is used for terms and facts. The topic or term is placed in the circle, and the information about the topic or term is written in the spokes. Consider for example, the first symbolizing task for details. It involves facts about immigration after the Civil War and asks students to use a map to represent these facts. This, of course, is a very precise way for students to symbolize such information. However, one or both of the graphic organizers in Figure 4.3 might have been used. For example "immigration after the Civil War" could be written in the circle and details about immigration written in the spokes.

The organizer at the bottom of Figure 4.3 is used for time sequences. If the information about immigration after the Civil War was conceptualized as a series of chronological events, the time sequence organizer could have been used. (A more detailed description of graphic organizers of this type can be found in Marzano, 2007, and Marzano & Pickering, 2005.)

Figure 4.4 depicts the type of graphic organizer commonly used with generalizations. The generalization is placed in the rectangle at the top and the examples of the generalization in the boxes below the top rectangle. For example, the generalization in Figure 4.2 about the commonalities between the past and present would be written in the rectangle. Examples would be written in the boxes below. Since principles involve relationships between variables, graphs and charts are typically used with this type of knowledge structure. For example, a student might create a graph representing the relationship between supply and demand for the task in Figure 4.1 involving this principle. A graph might show demand on one axis and supply on another. (For a more detailed discussion of these graphic organizers, see Marzano, 2007, and Marzano & Pickering, 2005.)

Figure 4.4   Graphic Organizers for Generalizations

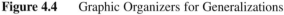

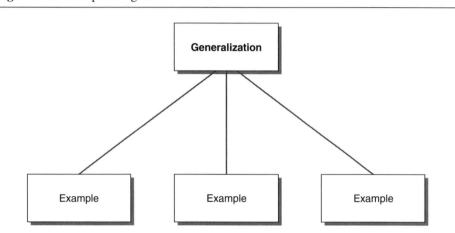

Symbolizing With Mental Procedures

Symbolizing as it relates to mental skills and processes typically involves designing a flow chart or diagram. Figure 4.5 depicts a common graphic organizer used to depict mental (and psychomotor) skills and processes.

Figure 4.5   Graphic Organizers for Skills and Processes

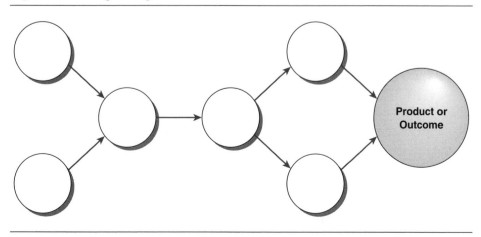

For example, a student might select the graphic organizer in Figure 4.5 to depict the skill of reading a newspaper article or the process of solving word problems. The causal relationships between the elements of these procedures are depicted in the relationships between the circles. The culminating event is a product or an outcome, such as comprehending the article or solving the word problem.

Symbolizing With Psychomotor Procedures

Symbolizing psychomotor procedures is similar to symbolizing mental procedures. It commonly involves flow charts and diagrams. In addition, it can involve pictures. To illustrate, a student might draw a diagram to depict the skill of striking a billiard ball. Similarly, a student might draw pictures to depict making S turns in skiing.

SUMMARY OF KEY POINTS FOR COMPREHENSION OBJECTIVES AND TASKS

Integrating Objectives and Tasks

- Require students to describe the critical versus noncritical elements of information
- Are more common with information than with mental or psychomotor procedures; when used with mental and psychomotor procedures they require students to explain the logic underlying the steps in a procedure.
- Use terms like the following: describe how or why, describe the key parts of, describe the effects, describe the relationship between, explain ways in which, make connections between, paraphrase, summarize
- Use extended written and oral constructed-response formats

Symbolizing Objectives and Tasks

- Require students to depict critical elements in some nonlinguistic or abstract form
- Use terms like the following: symbolize, depict, represent, illustrate, draw, show, use model, diagram, chart
- Use extended written and oral constructed-response formats along with graphic organizers, pictures, charts, graphs, tables, maps, and the like

CHAPTER FIVE

Analysis Objectives and Tasks

As described in Chapter 2, the analysis processes involve examining knowledge with the intent of generating new conclusions. There are five analysis processes: (1) matching, (2) classifying, (3) analyzing errors, (4) generalizing, and (5) specifying.

MATCHING

Matching involves identifying similarities and differences. Figure 5.1 presents matching objectives and tasks for the various domains of knowledge.

The verb *match* is rarely used in matching tasks. Most commonly, *compare* or *compare and contrast* are used. The following terms and phrases might also be used:

- Categorize
- Differentiate
- Discriminate
- Distinguish
- Sort
- Create an analogy
- Create a metaphor

It is important to note that matching can involve more than two examples of a specific type of knowledge. For example, a student demonstrates the ability to match by organizing individuals from history into two or more groups based on their similarities. The following task would elicit this type of matching:

We have been studying a number of individuals who were important historically for one reason or another. Organize these individuals into two or

Figure 5.1   Matching Objectives and Tasks

	Task	Objective	Knowledge Focus	Subject, Grade	Benchmark Statement
Information: Details: Terms, Facts, Time sequences	Compare the celebrations of Columbus Day in 1905 and 2005. How are they similar and how are they different?	The student will be able to identify the ways that celebrations of Columbus Day have changed and remained the same over time.	Details about Columbus Day in 1905 and 2005	Historical Understanding 7–8	Knows that history can be interpreted differently at different times according to newly discovered records or changing politics or viewpoints.
	We have been studying the terms *power* and *authority*. How are they alike and different?	The student will be able to name the similarities and differences between the terms *power* and *authority*.	The terms *power* and *authority*	Civics 3–5	Understands that power is simply the ability to direct or control something or someone while authority is power vested in people by custom, law, or the consent of the governed.
Information: Organizing Generalization	We have been studying patterns of migration, including seasonal migration. Identify the similarities and differences in human and animal migrations, especially with regard to the underlying causes.	The student will be able to describe the similarities and differences in the causes for human and animal migration.	Generalization about the causes of human and animal migration	Geography 6–8	Knows about migration and diffusion (e.g., the naturalization process of an immigrant; the spread of a disease through a population; global migration habits of plants and animals).
Information: Organizing Principle	What is common among conduction, convection and radiation in terms of the flow of heat energy? How do they differ?	The student will be able to identify what is common among the concepts of conduction, convection and radiation and how they differ from each other.	Principles regarding conduction, convection, and radiation	Science 6–8	Knows that heat energy flows through the processes of conduction, radiation, and convection from warm materials or regions to cool ones.

56

	Task	Objective	Knowledge Focus	Subject, Grade	Benchmark Statement
Mental Procedure: Skill	Describe how adding and multiplying are alike and how they are different.	The student will be able to describe how adding and multiplying are alike and how they differ.	The skills of adding and multiplying whole numbers	Math 3–5	Knows the elements of and relationships between addition, subtraction, multiplication, and division (e.g., addends can appear in any order; division is the reverse of multiplication).
	Compare situations when you would use a direct quote with those when you would paraphrase.	The student will be able to determine how to determine whether to use a direct quote or paraphrase.	The skills of using direct quotes and paraphrasing	Language Arts 6–8	Writes proper research papers (e.g., uses a thesis statement, uses a logical sequence, paraphrases or elaborates on ideas and connects them to related sources and topics, identifies validity and invalidity of information, addresses different points of view, converts information into forms such as charts and tables, seamlessly enhances work with quotations and citations, adapts researched material for presentation purposes).
Mental Procedure: Process	Describe how determining the validity of a primary source is similar to and different from determining the validity of a secondary source.	The student will be able to identify what is similar and different in determining the validity of a primary source and of a secondary source.	The process of determining the validity of primary sources and secondary sources	Language Arts 9–12	Evaluates the validity and reliability of primary and secondary sources by using awareness of the credibility and perspectives of the author and date of publication; use of logic, propaganda and bias; and comprehensiveness of evidence.

(Continued)

Figure 5.1 (Continued)

	Task	Objective	Knowledge Focus	Subject, Grade	Benchmark Statement
	Using specific examples, describe the difference between how you would take indirect and direct measurements.	The student will be able to compare the processes of direct and indirect measurements.	The processes of direct and indirect measurements	Math 6–8	Knows how to make basic indirect measurements (e.g., using grids or graphing paper to estimate area of irregular shapes).
Psychomotor Procedure: Skill	Identify how using a graphite pencil is similar to and different from using a charcoal pencil when sketching a person's face.	The student will be able to identify how using a graphite pencil is similar to and different from using a charcoal pencil for sketching a face.	The skills of using a graphite pencil and a charcoal pencil in a specific situation	Visual Arts K–4	Understands the differences between art tools (e.g., paint, clay, film), techniques (e.g., layering, shading, size variation), and processes (e.g., tinting in photography, firing in pottery).
	Describe how hitting a baseball that is placed on a tee is similar to and different from hitting a baseball thrown by a pitcher.	The student will be able to identify the similarities and differences between hitting a baseball on a tee and hitting a baseball thrown by a pitcher.	The skills of hitting a baseball from a tee and hitting a thrown baseball	Physical Education 7–8	Knows how to condition and train for select physical activities.
Psychomotor Procedure: Process	Contrast the approaches used to control speed and direction in snowboarding with those used in skateboarding or skiing as it compares to rollerblading.	The student will be able to identify the similarities and differences between two closely related sports, such as snowboarding and skateboarding.	The processes of snowboarding, skateboarding, skiing, and rollerblading	Physical Education 7–8	Understands sophistication in movement associated with highly skilled athletes (e.g., what makes a successful vs. an unsuccessful play in football).
	Select two specific types of dances we have been studying, such as tap and ballet. How are they similar and how are they different?	The student will be able to identify the similarities and differences between two types of dances.	The processes of performing specific types of dances	Dance 9–12	Understands advanced movements associated with various types of dances.

more groups and explain how the individuals within each group are similar. Also explain how the individuals are different from group to group:

Alexander Graham Bell

Galileo

George Washington Carver

Louis Pasteur

Amelia Earhart

Sally Ride

John Glenn

Henry Ford

Eric the Red

Ferdinand Magellan

Jacques Cartier

Martin Luther King, Jr.

This example illustrates that what is typically thought of as a categorizing task is considered matching in the New Taxonomy. This is because categorizing as exemplified in the foregoing task involves sorting elements into like categories based on their characteristics. As described in Chapter 2, classifying in the New Taxonomy focuses on superordinate and subordinate categories, whereas matching focuses on similarities and differences.

Matching can also employ an analogy format like the following:

Explain how the relationship between a bone and a skeleton is similar to and different from the relationship between a word and a sentence.

Analogy formats require students to identify how a relationship between one pair of elements is similar to the relationship between a second pair of elements. In this case, it is how the relationship between a bone and a skeleton is similar to the relationship between a word and a sentence.

Finally, matching tasks can also employ a metaphor format like the following:

Explain the following metaphor: Helen Keller was the Frederick Douglass of her family.

To complete this task, a student must determine how Helen Keller and Frederick Douglass are alike at an abstract level, since they bear little resemblance at a concrete level. This is the essence of a metaphor, identifying abstract similarities when there are few or no concrete similarities.

All the example tasks in Figure 5.1 use short or extended written or oral constructed-response formats. As a guide to completing matching tasks, the graphic organizers in Figure 5.2 are commonly used.

Figure 5.2   Graphic Organizers for Matching

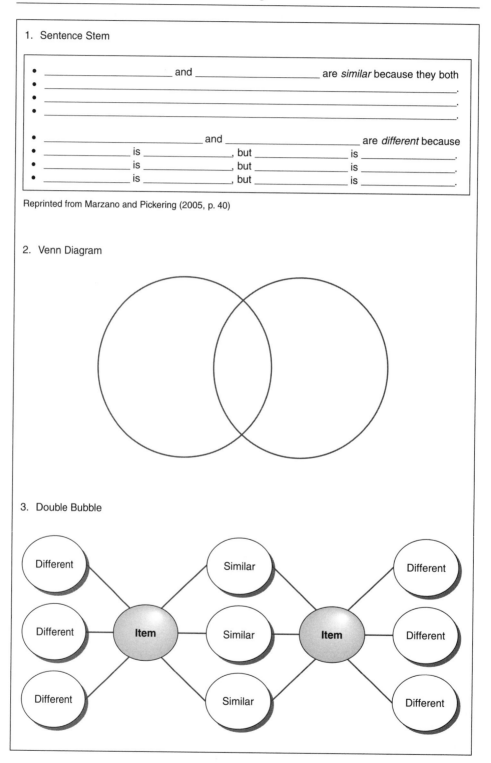

1. Sentence Stem

  - _____ and _____ are *similar* because they both
  - _____ .
  - _____ .
  - _____ .

  - _____ and _____ are *different* because
  - _____ is _____ , but _____ is _____ .
  - _____ is _____ , but _____ is _____ .
  - _____ is _____ , but _____ is _____ .

Reprinted from Marzano and Pickering (2005, p. 40)

2. Venn Diagram

3. Double Bubble

Different   Similar   Different

Different   Item   Similar   Item   Different

Different   Similar   Different

4. Comparison Matrix

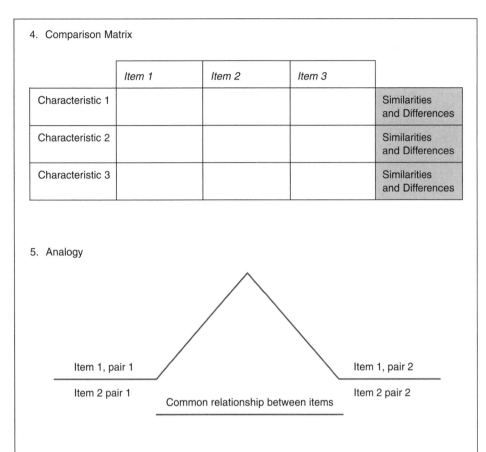

	Item 1	Item 2	Item 3	
Characteristic 1				Similarities and Differences
Characteristic 2				Similarities and Differences
Characteristic 3				Similarities and Differences

5. Analogy

Item 1, pair 1   Item 1, pair 2

Item 2 pair 1   Item 2 pair 2

Common relationship between items

6. Metaphor

Characteristics of Item 1	Common General Characteristics	Characteristics of Item 2

Source: Adapted from *Building Academic Vocabulary: Teacher's Manual* (pp. 40, 43, 44, 50, 52). Marzano, Robert J., & Pickering, Debra J. Alexandria, VA: ASCD, 2005.

For a detailed description of the graphic organizers in Figure 5.2, see Marzano and Pickering (2005). The first graphic organizer is a sentence stem. Sentence stems provide students with explicit guidance regarding how to describe similarities and differences between items. To illustrate, assume a student was matching the sun and the moon. In the top portion of the sentence stem, the terms *sun* and *moon* are recorded along with a description of how they are similar. The student might write,

- They are both bodies in space.
- They both have an influence on the earth.
- They both provide light.

The bottom portion of the stem is reserved for differences. There the student might write,
The sun and moon are different because

- The sun is about 93 million miles from earth, but the moon is about 250,000 miles away.
- The sun is made up of gases, but the moon is made up of rocks.
- The sun influences temperature and seasons, but the moon influences tides.

The second organizer is the Venn diagram. Each circle represents one of the items being matched. Similarities between items are written in the area of intersection between the two circles. Differences are recorded in the parts of each circle that do not intersect.

The third organizer in Figure 5.2 is the double bubble. It was popularized by Hyerle (1996). Similarities are recorded in the bubbles between the two items. For example, three similarities between the sun and the moon would be recorded in the three bubbles in the middle. Differences would be recorded in the bubbles on the far right and far left.

The fourth organizer is the comparison matrix. The columns represent the items to be compared; the rows represent the characteristics on which they are compared. To illustrate, consider the matching task in Figure 5.1 for principles. It asks students to compare principles regarding conduction, convection and radiation. These items would be placed as the column headings in the comparison matrix. Next, students (or the teacher) would identify characteristics on which to compare the three. Those characteristics might be (1) amount of heat generated, (2) method of heat transfer, and (3) use in cooking. These would be placed in the rows of the comparison matrix. In the appropriate cells, students would then record the similarities and differences between conduction, convection, and radiation on these characteristics.

The fifth organizer is used for analogies. As shown in Figure 5.3, the first pair of elements in the analogy is written above and below the left side. The second pair of elements in the analogy is written above and below the line on the right side. The common relationship between the two pairs is written on the line below the triangle.

Figure 5.3   Analogy Graphic Organizer

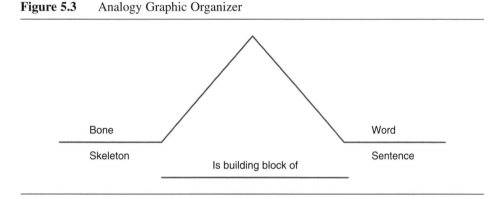

The sixth organizer is used with metaphors. The two terms in the metaphor are written at the tops of the first and third columns. Explicit characteristics for both terms are written in the rows for their respective terms. The middle column articulates the abstract commonalities between the two terms in the metaphor. This is depicted in Figure 5.4.

Figure 5.4   Metaphor Graphic Organizer

Characteristics of Item 1	Common General Characteristics	Characteristics of Item 2
Frederick Douglass		**Helen Keller**
Was a slave as a young boy	Had a rough beginning	Got sick as a baby, which left her deaf and blind
Learned to read and write anyway	Achieved goals even when difficult	Learned how to read Braille and write; also went to college
Wrote books and gave speeches against slavery	Worked to help other people who suffered like they did.	Through speech tours and writing, inspired others to overcome their disabilities

Source: From *Building Academic Vocabulary: Teacher's Manual* (p 52). Marzano, Robert J., & Pickering, Debra J. Alexandria, VA: ASCD, 2005.

Here the metaphor involves Frederick Douglass and Helen Keller. On the surface, they bear little resemblance. Frederick Douglass was a slave; Helen Keller got sick as a baby, which left her deaf and blind. However at an abstract level, these two characteristics are related; they demonstrate that both Frederick Douglass and Helen Keller had rough beginnings. It is the abstract relationships articulated in the middle column that constitute the metaphoric link between the two items.

Matching With Information

Matching tasks for details involve identifying the manner in which terms, facts or time sequences are similar to and different from related structures. For example, the first matching task for details requires students to determine the similarities and differences between facts pertaining to the Columbus Day celebrations of 1905 and 2005. Matching tasks for organizing ideas involve identifying how one principle or generalization is similar to and different from other generalizations and principles. For example, the matching task for generalizations requires students to describe similarities and differences between characteristics of human migration and animal migration.

Matching With Mental Procedures

Matching tasks for mental skills involve identifying how two or more skills are similar and different in terms of their component parts. For example, the first matching task for mental skills requires students to describe the similarities and differences between the skills of addition and multiplication. Matching tasks for mental processes involve identifying how two or more processes are similar and different in terms of their component parts. For example, the first matching task for mental processes requires students to describe the similarities and differences between the processes of determining the validity of primary and secondary sources.

Matching With Psychomotor Procedures

Matching tasks for psychomotor skills involve identifying how two or more physical skills are similar and different in terms of the steps they involve. For example, the first matching task for psychomotor skills requires students to describe the similarities and differences between the skills of using a graphite pencil and a charcoal pencil when sketching. Matching tasks for psychomotor processes involve identifying how two or more physical processes are similar and different in terms of the steps they involve. For example, the first matching task for psychomotor processes requires students to describe the similarities and differences between the processes of snowboarding and skateboarding or between the processes of skiing and rollerblading.

CLASSIFYING

Classifying as defined in the New Taxonomy goes beyond organizing items into groups or categories. Rather, classifying involves identifying the superordinate category in which knowledge belongs as well as the subordinate categories (if any) for knowledge. Figure 5.5 presents classifying objectives and tasks for the various domains of knowledge.

As illustrated in the right-most column of Figure 5.5, classifying is sometimes explicit in benchmark statements. To illustrate, consider the row of Figure 5.5 that addresses informational details. The benchmark statement in this second example of classifying details addresses knowledge of types of regions. Implicit in such knowledge is the process of classifying specific locations within superordinate categories, such as formal regions, functional regions and perceptual regions. As described in the previous discussion of matching, classifying in the New Taxonomy involves identification of superordinate and subordinate categories as opposed to identifying similarities and differences only.

The term *classify* is frequently employed in classifying tasks as well as terms and phrases like the following:

- Organize
- Sort
- Identify a broader category
- Identify categories
- Identify different types

The most common format for classifying tasks is short or extended written and oral constructed-response formats. Commonly, graphic organizers like those shown in Figure 5.6 are used as aids and guides in classifying tasks.

The first organizer in Figure 5.6 is used when a classifying task involves sorting elements into superordinate categories. The superordinate categories form the column heads, and elements are listed under their appropriate superordinate category. This is depicted in Figure 5.7.

Here the three columns are titled Art Materials, Art Techniques and Art Processes. In addition to this organizer, students would be given the following list of elements, all relating to art: paint, clay, overlapping, shading, varying size and color, adding in sculpture, subtracting in sculpture, casting jewelry, charcoal, pencil, wood, collage, mural, stippling, glaze, mixing color, and constructing jewelry. Students would be asked to sort these art elements into their respective superordinate categories.

The second organizer in Figure 5.6 is used when the classifying task involves identifying subordinate categories. Subordinate categories are placed in the circles below the element that is the focus of the classifying task. This is depicted in Figure 5.8.

(*Text continues on page 71*)

Figure 5.5   Classifying Objectives and Tasks

	Task	Objective	Knowledge Focus	Subject, Grade	Benchmark Statement
Information: Details: Terms, Facts, Time sequences	We have been studying how food provides protein, fat and carbohydrates and fiber, vitamins and minerals. Organize the following foods into each of three lists, showing how you think they rank for relative amounts of protein, fat, and vitamins. • Fruits • Vegetables • Butter • Steak • Pasta	The student will be able to classify food by its relative amount of protein, fat, and vitamins.	Details about the amount of fat, protein, and vitamins in food	Health 9–12	Knows the relative nutritional value of different foods.
	Select two cities we have been studying and describe the likely formal, functional, and perceptual regions they share.	The student will be able to classify specific cities by the characteristics they share as regions (formal, functional, and perceptual).	Details about specific cities	Geography 6–8	Understands that regions can be formal (e.g., school districts, states of the United States, different countries), functional (e.g., the marketing area of a local newspaper, the "fanshed" of a professional sports team), and perceptual (e.g., the Bible Belt in the United States, the Riviera in southern France).
Information: Organizing Generalization	We have been studying trends as they relate to weather phenomena, but trends have also been studied relative to demographic data, even fashion. What do such trend analyses have in common? How would we describe them in more general terms? How do these attempts differ from each other in terms of what they might describe or accomplish?	The student will be able to classify trends in terms of the types of data on which they depend (physical, demographic, social) and the phenomena they attempt to predict.	Characteristics of trends for different types of data	Science 9–12	Understands the criteria that scientific explanations must meet to be considered valid (e.g., consistency with evidence about nature, making accurate predictions about systems, be logical, respect the rules of evidence, be open to criticism, report methods and procedures, make a commitment to making knowledge public).

	Task	Objective	Knowledge Focus	Subject, Grade	Benchmark Statement
Information: Organizing Principle	The muscle overload principle forms a part of what larger set of principles related to physical exercise? What are some categories of the muscle overload principle in action?	The student will be able to identify the muscle overload principle as important for strength training.	A principle regarding muscle overload	Physical Education 7–8	Knows principles of training that enhance fitness (e.g., threshold, overload, specificity, frequency, intensity, duration, and mode of exercise).
Mental Procedure: Skill	Correcting for spelling is a task that is part of what collection of important skills? What other skills are commonly used at the same time?	The student will be able to classify spell-checking as among the proofreading and editing skills needed to prepare written work for publishing.	The skill of correcting spelling errors	Language Arts 3–5	Uses strategies to edit and publish written work (e.g., corrects mistakes in grammar, punctuation, capitalization, and spelling at an appropriate level; uses reference materials; considers page format [paragraphs, margins, indentations, titles]; selects presentation format according to purpose; incorporates visual elements; uses available technology).
	We have learned that other cultures use different gestures when speaking. What is the broader term for a type of communication that includes gestures? What are other examples of this category?	The student will be able to identify gestures as an example of nonverbal communication.	The skill of using gestures as a form of communication	Foreign Language K–4	Uses and understands appropriate nonverbal cues and body language (e.g., clarifies verbal messages, engages a listener's attention, expresses humor).
Mental Procedure: Process	We have been learning what to do when crossing the street and also what to do in the event of a fire or earthquake. What kinds of rules are these examples of? What other rules are there like this?	The student will be able to identify certain rules as those that are established and followed for personal safety.	The process of personal safety	Health PreK	Knows the routines to follow in emergency situations (e.g., fire drills, calling 911, running from or screaming at someone trying to hurt you).

(Continued)

Figure 5.5 (Continued)

	Task	Objective	Knowledge Focus	Subject, Grade	Benchmark Statement
	To what type of mathematical computations do the commutative, associative, and distributive properties apply? What is an example of each?	The student will be able to identify that certain operations are used with rational numbers.	Mental processes performed on rational numbers	Math 6–8	Knows operations with rational numbers (e.g., distributive property, commutative and associative properties of addition and multiplication, inverse properties, identity properties).
Psychomotor Procedure: Skill	When using thermometers, rulers and graduated cylinders, what type of skills are we engaged in? What are other examples of this type of skill?	The student will be able to classify tools and simple equipment as those used in gathering data.	The skills of using specific types of tools to collect data	Science 3–5	Gathers scientific data using simple tools and equipment (e.g., thermometers, microscopes, calculators, balances, graduated cylinders).
	What types of dance skills are following and mirroring? What other examples are there of these types of skills?	The student will be able to classify skills as common in partner dance.	The skills of partner dancing	Dance K–4	Uses partner skills such as leading and following as well as copying and mirroring.
Psychomotor Procedure: Process	What is the category of strategies used in playing tennis, ping-pong and badminton; how are these different from invasion games?	The student will be able to classify strategies as common to net games as opposed to invasion games.	The process of playing a net game	Physical Education 3–5	Uses beginning strategies for net and invasion games (e.g., keeping the ball going or away from opponent in a racket sport, dribbling the ball in basketball).
	We have been practicing a number of musical pieces over the past few weeks, each of which uses crescendo. Describe some of the categories of crescendo these pieces might fall into.	The student will be able to identify the various categories of crescendo.	The process of music performance	Music 9–12	Performs at an intermediate level (e.g., attends to phrasing and interpretation, performs various meters and rhythms in a variety of keys) a variety of musical pieces with expression (e.g., appropriate dynamics, phrasing, rubato).

Figure 5.6   Graphic Organizers for Generalizing

1. Superordinate Categories

Superordinate Category 1	*Superordinate Category 2*	*Superordinate Category 3*

2. Subordinate Categories

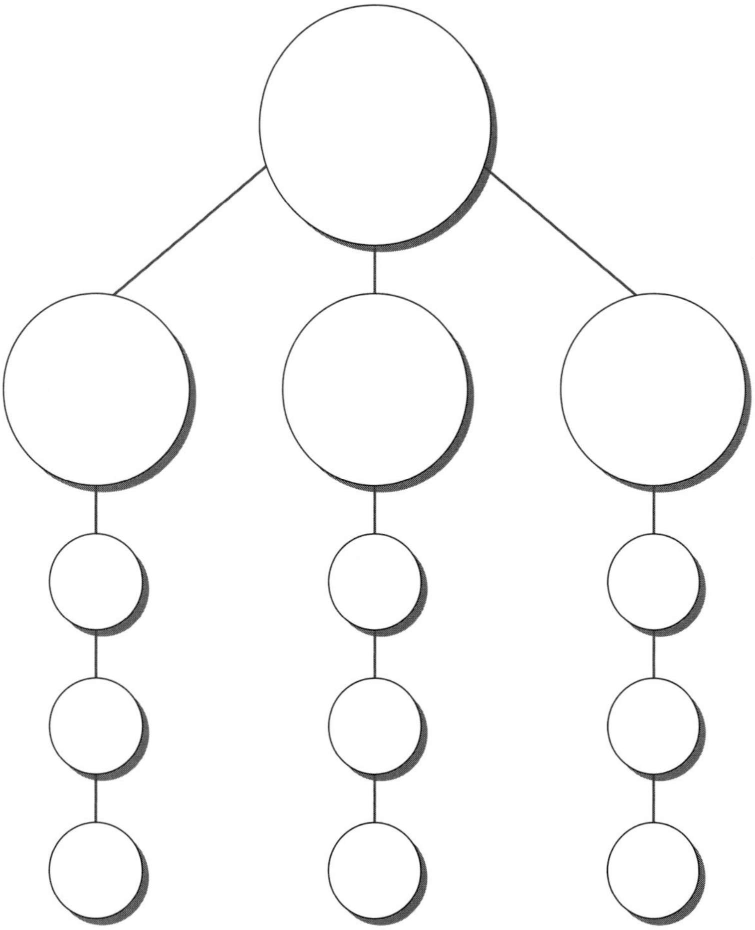

Figure 5.7   Graphic Organizers for Superordinate Categories

Art Materials	Art Techniques	Art Processes

Figure 5.8   Graphic Organizer for Subordinate Categories

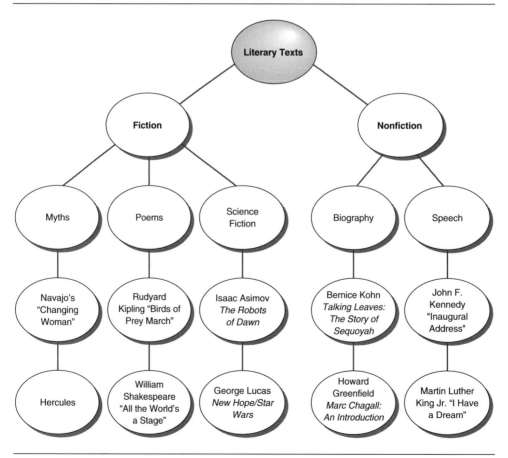

In Figure 5.8, students have been asked to identify various types of fiction and nonfiction, both of which are subsumed under the larger category of types of literary texts.

Classifying With Information

Classifying tasks for details involve the identification of superordinate and subordinate categories. For example, the first classifying task for details requires students to classify fruits, vegetables, butter, steak, and pasta into three categories: protein, fat, and vitamins. This requires students to sort each food type into predetermined superordinate categories in their proper order based on the extent to which these food types contain protein, fat, and vitamins. It is important to note that this task requires a different type of thinking than would be required if the task simply was to organize these food types into categories of their own choosing. The later is simple matching involving similarities and differences between food types. The task in Figure 5.6 requires organizing elements into predetermined superordinate categories. Classifying tasks for details more commonly involve superordinate categories than subordinate categories because of the specificity of details.

Classifying tasks for organizing ideas involve superordinate and subordinate categories. For example, the classifying task for principles requires students to identify the superordinate category for a principle involving muscle overload. This task demonstrates that classifying tasks can be completed with a relatively short response on the part of students. Here students would simply have to state that the principle of overload belongs to a bigger (i.e., superordinate) category of principles regarding strength training and explain why. The brevity of the required response, however, does not detract from its cognitive complexity.

Classifying With Mental Procedures

Classifying tasks for mental skills involve the identification of superordinate and subordinate categories. For example, the first classifying task for mental skills requires students to classify the skill of correcting spelling errors as belonging to the superordinate category of skills involved in proofreading and editing. Conversely, students could have been asked to identify subordinate categories of spelling errors. Classifying tasks for mental processes involve both superordinate and subordinate categories. The first classifying task for mental processes requires students to classify specific rules as belonging to the superordinate category of personal safety. Conversely, students could have been asked to identify subordinate categories of personal safety.

Classifying With Psychomotor Procedures

Classifying tasks for psychomotor skills and processes involve identifying superordinate and subordinate categories for specific physical skills. For example, the first classifying task for psychomotor skills requires students to identify the superordinate category of the psychomotor skills of using thermometers, rulers, and graduated cylinders. The first classifying task for psychomotor processes requires students to identify the superordinate category of net games. Had the superordinate category been given first, the classifying task would have involved identifying examples of net games, such as tennis, Ping-Pong and badminton.

ANALYZING ERRORS

Analyzing errors involves identifying factual or logical errors in knowledge or processing errors in the execution of knowledge. Figure 5.9 depicts objectives and tasks for analyzing errors across the domains of knowledge.

The verb *analyze errors* can be used in analyzing errors objectives and tasks. Other terms and phrases include the following:

- Identify problems
- Identify issues
- Identify misunderstandings
- Assess
- Critique
- Diagnose
- Evaluate
- Edit
- Revise

The common format for analyzing errors is short or extended written or oral constructed-response formats. In addition, more structured formats might be employed. To illustrate, consider the following task:

John knows that you are most likely to get a sunburn if you are out in the sun between 11:00 a.m. and 1:00 p.m. He asks six of his friends why this is so. They each give him a different answer. Identify which of the answers are wrong and explain the errors made in each case:

Answer 1: We are slightly closer to the sun at noon than in the morning or afternoon.

Answer 2: More "burn" will be produced by the noon sun than by the morning or afternoon sun.

Answer 3: When the sun's rays fall straight down (directly) on a surface, more energy is received than when they fall indirectly on the surface.

(*Text continues on page 77*)

Figure 5.9   Analyzing Errors Objectives and Tasks

	Task	Objective	Knowledge Focus	Subject, Grade	Benchmark Statement
Information: Details: Terms, Facts, Time sequences	Review campaign literature of competing candidates to determine whether a candidate has simplified an issue in ways that could mislead anyone who is not familiar with the details.	The student will be able to determine the accuracy of content presented in a persuasive argument, such as a political speech.	Details about specific candidates for public office	Civics 9–12	Understands the use of logical validity, factual accuracy, emotional appeal, distorted evidence and appeals to bias and how they affect the validity of historical and contemporary political communication (e.g., Lincoln's "House Divided," Sojourner Truth's "Ain't I a Woman?," Chief Joseph's "I Shall Fight No More Forever," Martin Luther King, Jr.'s "I Have a Dream," campaign advertisements, political cartoons).
	Your friend argues that the mountain range right outside our city was caused by a massive storm centuries ago. Based on what you know about earth processes, could this story be true? Why or why not?	The student will be able to determine the accuracy of specific information based on knowledge of earth's physical processes.	Details regarding the earth's physical processes	Geography 3–5	Identifies patterns on the landscape created by physical processes (e.g., the timberline in mountainous regions, the vegetation on the exposed and protected sides of a mountain range).
Information: Organizing Generalization	We have been studying the early American novel. The characters in these early works have been described as flat and unidimensional. Identify some of the errors or inconsistencies in this position.	The student will be able to identify what is plausible and implausible about the characters in a given genre.	A generalization about the characters in a given genre	Language Arts 9–12	Understands features of character development in literature (e.g., differences between the protagonist and antagonist, flat vs. full characters, changes in characters, the importance of a character's actions and motives).

(Continued)

73

Figure 5.9 (Continued)

	Task	Objective	Knowledge Focus	Subject, Grade	Benchmark Statement
Information: Organizing Principle	The story we just read argues that humans were responsible for the extinction of the dinosaurs. Based on your understanding of the earth's early history, identify the problems with this argument.	The student will be able to identify the fallacy of an argument based on an understanding of fossil evidence.	Principles regarding fossil evidence	Science 6–8	Knows how the age, history and changing life forms of the earth can be determined by fossils and the area around them and how this evidence can be compromised by the folding, breaking and uplifting of layers.
Mental Procedure: Skill	The graph presented to you shows an extreme rise and fall in a stock's price over the past 2 months. Yet the accompanying data used to develop this graph indicate a change by a few dollars over the period, which the graph correctly indicates. What created the misimpression?	The student will be able to identify flaws in graph presentation based on skill at interpreting the x and y axes.	The skill of reading a specific type of graph	Math 6–8	Understands that the same set of data can be represented using a variety of tables, graphs, and symbols to convey different messages (e.g., variation in scale can alter a visual message).
	You've imported a table from a spreadsheet document into the paper you are writing, but the table loses some formatting and overruns the page margins. What is the likely cause of this error?	The student will be able to diagnose errors in data formatting based on an understanding of the steps used to import data.	The skill of importing a table from a spreadsheet to a Word file	Technology 6–8	Knows the elements and uses of spreadsheets (e.g., cells, row and column; formulas used to immediately update data; spreadsheets used in print and electronic form for purposes such as to tracking business profit and loss) Uses sophisticated features of computer programs (e.g., clip art, spell-checker, thesaurus, word count).

	Task	Objective	Knowledge Focus	Subject, Grade	Benchmark Statement
Mental Procedure: Process	You've just finished making a presentation to the class on a book that you read about the Civil War. One of the questions a fellow student asks is, "Why did you choose that book for your presentation?" Does that suggest that you made in error in putting together your presentation? How might you have anticipated the question?	The student will be able to recognize errors in oral presentation through a consideration of audience expectations.	The process of designing and delivering an oral presentation	Language Arts 6–8	Presents orally expressing a clear point of view (e.g., uses organizational patterns such as outlines, previews, introduction, body, transitions, and conclusion; uses evidence and arguments to support opinions; uses visual aids).
	You've exchanged papers in class to check one another's work. For one problem that asks for the median of a list of integers, you see that 10.25 is the answer the student provided. How do you know this is an error without even doing the calculation first? What seems a likely explanation for this error?	The student will be able to identify errors related to median, mean and mode based on an understanding of the processes used to calculate them.	The process of solving problems regarding central tendency	Math 6–8	Knows measures of central tendency (i.e., mean, mode, median).
Psychomotor Procedure: Skill	Videotape your execution of a skill that you want to improve. Review the tape in slow motion to identify any incorrect body position or movement.	The student will be able to identify sport performance errors based on an understanding of sport-specific skills.	A specific physical skill of the student's choice	Physical Education 9–12	Uses sophisticated skills in physical activities (e.g., swimming, ballet, mountain biking, individual and team sports).

(Continued)

Figure 5.9 (Continued)

	Task	Objective	Knowledge Focus	Subject, Grade	Benchmark Statement
	Videotape your performance on an instrument of your choice. Identify errors in a specific aspect of your technique and explain how you might address these errors.	The student will be able to identify technical errors in technique for a chosen instrument.	Specific techniques for playing an instrument of the student's choice	Music 6–8	Expressly and accurately performs on a classroom instrument a variety of pieces that include modest ranges and changes of tempo, key and meter.
Psychomotor Procedure: Process	Watch the video of a judged competition in a sport that interests you. Keep your own score for each competitor, provide a rationale for the score, and attempt to reconcile your scores against the judges' scores or final rankings. Do you think the judges made any errors in their ranking?	The student will be able to identify errors in competitive performance of a specific sport based on knowledge of the movement elements required.	A specific sport of the student's choice	Physical Education 3–6	Uses appropriate movement sequences for selected games, sports and dances (e.g., combining steps to perform certain dances; combining running, stopping, throwing, catching, and hitting for baseball).
	Select a sport, art, or craft for which you consider yourself at least at the intermediate level. Browse the web for a site that offers tips and techniques and determine whether or not they seem valid based on your experience.	The student will be able to determine whether there are errors in the description of a technique or process based on an understanding of the technique or process.	A specific sport, art, or craft of the student's choice	Visual Arts 9–12 Physical Education 7–8	Completes artwork with sufficient competence and confidence (e.g. technique, process) with the goal of carrying out intention Understands sophistication in movement associated with highly skilled athletes (e.g., moves that lead to successful serves and passes as opposed to unsuccessful serves and passes in volleyball).

Answer 4: When the sun is directly overhead, its rays pass through less atmosphere than when it is lower in the sky.

Answer 5: The air is usually warmer at noon than at any other time of the day.

Answer 6: The ultraviolet rays of sunlight are mainly responsible for sunburn.

The foregoing example involves information. The following example involves the mental process of using the word-processing software WordPerfect:

Robert plans to perform the following steps to write a composition using WordPerfect. Identify what will go wrong if he carries out the following steps exactly as stated:

1. When he gets into WordPerfect, he will begin by clicking on the CENTER command on the bar at the top of the page.

2. He will type in his three-paragraph composition.

3. When he is done, he will click on the small x in the upper right-hand corner of the screen.

4. The next day he will reopen WordPerfect and print out his composition.

Analyzing Errors With Information

In terms of details, analyzing errors tasks involve determining the extent to which information is reasonable, given what the student already knows about the topic. For example, the first analyzing errors task for details involves information about a specific candidate for public office. Students must determine possible errors in the candidate's position on a specific issue. Relative to organizing ideas, analyzing errors tasks involve determining whether statements regarding a generalization or a principle are logical. For example, the analyzing errors task regarding the generalization about characters in a specific genre asks students to identify inconsistencies or errors in this position.

Tasks employing analyzing errors for information typically require knowledge of different types of errors that might be made. Figure 5.10 presents four categories of such errors.

Other than the types of logical errors listed in Figure 5.10, analyzing errors requires knowledge of how to present and defend a claim. This is depicted in Figure 5.11.

Figure 5.11 provides a generic framework for providing support for a claim. Students do not have to understand the technical aspects of grounds, backing, and qualifiers (such as their names and defining characteristics). However, they should be aware that valid claims should be supported (grounds), this support should be explained (backing), and exceptions to the claim should be identified (qualifiers).

Figure 5.10   Four Categories of Logical Errors

1. *Faulty logic* can occur in seven different ways:

   A. *Contradiction*—presenting conflicting information. If a politician runs on a platform supporting term limits, then votes against an amendment that would set term limits, that politician has committed the error of contradiction.

   B. *Accident*—failing to recognize than an argument is based on an exception to a rule. For example, if a student concludes that the principal always goes to dinner at a fancy restaurant on Fridays because he or she sees him at one on a given Friday which just happens to be his birthday, that student has committed the error of accident.

   C. *False cause*—confusing a temporal (time) order of events with causality or oversimplifying the reasons behind some event or occurrence. For example, if a person concludes that the war in Vietnam ended because of the antiwar protests, he or she is guilty of ascribing a false cause. The antiwar protests might have had something to do with the cessation of the war, but there were also many other interacting causes.

   D. *Begging the question*—making a claim and then arguing for the claim by using statements that are simply the equivalent of the original claim. For example, if a person says that product x is the best detergent on the market and then backs up this statement by simply saying that it is superior to other detergents, he or she is begging the question.

   E. *Evading the issue*—changing the topic to avoid addressing the issue. For example, a person is evading the issue if he or she begins talking about the evils of the news media when asked by a reporter about an alleged involvement in fraudulent banking procedures.

   F. *Arguing from ignorance*—arguing that a claim is justified simply because its opposite has not been proven true. For example, if a person argues that there is no life on other planets because there has been no proof of such existence, he or she is arguing from ignorance.

   G. *Composition–division*—asserting something about a whole that is really only true of its parts is *composition*; on the flip side, *division* is asserting about all of the parts something that is generally, but not always, true of the whole. For example, if a person asserts that Republicans are corrupt because one Republican is found to be corrupt, he or she is committing the error of composition. If a person states that a particular Democrat supports big government simply because Democrats are generally known for supporting government programs, he or she is committing the error of division.

2. *Attacks* can occur in three ways:

   A. *Poisoning the well*—being so completely committed to a position that you explain away absolutely everything that is offered in opposition to your position. This type of attack represents a person's unwillingness to consider anything that may contradict his or her opinion. For example, if a political candidate has only negative things to say about an opponent, he or she is poisoning the well.

   B. *Arguing against the person*—rejecting a claim using derogatory facts (real or alleged) about the person who is making the claim. If a person argues against another person's position on taxation by making reference to poor moral character, he or she is arguing against the person.

   C. *Appealing to force*—using threats to establish the validity of a claim. If your landlord threatens to evict you because you disagree with him or her on an upcoming election issue, he or she is appealing to force.

3. *Weak reference* occurs in five ways:

   A. *Sources that reflect biases*—consistently accepting information that supports what we already believe to be true, or consistently rejecting information that goes against what we believe to be true. For example, a person is guilty of bias if he or she believes that a person has committed a crime and will not even consider DNA evidence indicating that the individual is innocent.

B. *Sources that lack credibility*—using a source that is not reputable for a given topic. Determining credibility can be subjective, but there are some characteristics that most people agree damage credibility, such as when a source is known to be biased or has little knowledge of the topic. A person is guilty of using a source that lacks credibility when he or she backs up a belief that the government has a conspiracy to ruin the atmosphere by citing a tabloid journal known for sensational stories that are fabricated.

C. *Appealing to authority*—invoking authority as the last word on an issue. If a person says, "Socialism is evil" and supports this claim by saying the governor said so, he or she is appealing to authority.

D. *Appealing to the people*—attempting to justify a claim based on its popularity. For example, if a girl tells her parents she should have a pierced belly button because everyone else has one, she is appealing to the people.

E. *Appealing to emotion*—using a so-called sob story as proof for a claim. For example, if someone uses the story of a tragic accident in his or her life as a means to convince people to agree with his or her opinion on war, she is appealing to emotion.

4. **Misinformation** occurs in two different ways:

1. *Confusing the facts*—using information that seems to be factual but that has been changed in such a way that it is no longer accurate. For example, a person is confusing the facts if he or she backs up a claim by describing an event but leaving out important facts or mixing up the temporal order of the events.

2. *Misapplying a concept or generalization*—misunderstanding or wrongly applying a concept or generalization to support a claim. For example, if someone argues that a talk-show host should be arrested for libel after making a critical remark, the person has misapplied the concept of libel.

Source: Marzano & Kendall (2007)

Figure 5.11   Framework for Supporting a Claim

Grounds: Once a claim is made, it should be supported by grounds. Depending on the type of claim made, grounds may be composed of

*   Matters of common knowledge
*   Expert opinion
*   Experimental evidence
*   Other information considered factual

Backing: Backing establishes the validity of grounds and discusses them in depth.

Qualifiers: Not all grounds support their claims with the same degree of certainty. Consequently, qualifiers state the degree of certainty for the claim or exceptions to it or both.

Source: Marzano & Kendall (2007).

Analyzing Errors With Mental Procedures

In terms of mental skills and processes, analyzing errors tasks involve identifying errors that someone is making or has made while executing a mental procedure. For example, the first analyzing errors task for mental skills involves reading a specific type of graph. The first analyzing errors task for mental processes involves the process of designing and delivering an oral presentation. When procedures are involved (mental or psychomotor), the emphasis is not on logical errors, as is the case with information (details and organizing ideas). Rather the emphasis is on identifying any errors or bugs in the execution of the procedure.

Analyzing Errors With Psychomotor Procedures

Analyzing errors tasks for psychomotor procedures follow the same pattern as analyzing errors tasks for mental procedures. They involve the identification of errors someone has made or is making while carrying out a psychomotor skill or process. For example, the first analyzing errors task for psychomotor skills involves a specific physical skill of the student's choice. The first analyzing errors task for psychomotor processes involves the process of playing a sport of the student's choice.

GENERALIZING

The analysis skill of generalizing involves inferring new generalizations and principles from information that is known or stated. Figure 5.12 depicts generalizing objectives and tasks across the domains of knowledge.

The term *generalize* can be used in generalizing tasks along with terms and phrases like the following:

- What conclusions can be drawn
- What inferences can be made
- Create a generalization
- Create a principle
- Create a rule
- Trace the development of
- Form conclusions

The most common format for generalizing tasks is short or extended written or oral constructed-response formats. These tasks might be relatively unstructured, like those in Figure 5.12, or they might be highly structured as in the following two examples:

(*Text continues on page 85*)

Figure 5.12 Generalizing Objectives and Tasks

	Task	Objective	Knowledge Focus	Subject, Grade	Benchmark Statement
Information: Details: Terms, Facts, Time sequences	We have been studying settlements from ancient times to modern. Based upon what you know about two specific settlements, what generalizations can you make about where people tend to establish settlements and why?	The student will be able to construct and defend a generalization about why human settlements appear where they do.	Details about specific settlements	Geography 6–8	Knows that physical and human distributions occur with respect to spatial and human patterns, arrangements, and associations (e.g., why some areas are more densely settled, patterns in the kind and number of links between settlements).
	Messages about health products can be helpful, alerting us to their usefulness, how they are best used, and their side effects. But each health product is made by a company with a specific view of health. Select one health product and find out details about the company that produced it. What generalizations can you make about the health product based on the information about the company?	The student will be able to make generalizations about the influence of sources of information on the validity and usefulness of the information presented.	Details about specific sources of information	Health 6–8	Knows how messages from the media, friends and other local sources can impact health practices (e.g., health fads, advertising, misconceptions about health).
Information: Organizing Generalization	We have seen evidence for a number of generalizations about history and geography. For example, the rocky interior of ancient Greece and easy access to the Mediterranean Sea provide support for the generalization that the geography of a region can have a significant impact on a country's future. The early United States, whose land teemed with resources and the	The student will be able to develop generalizations about how knowledge of the past can be used to better understand possible consequences of present actions.	Generalizations about history and geography	Geography 6–8	Understands how physical and human geographic factors influence major events and movements in history (e.g., the course and outcome of battles and wars, the slave trade in the United States because of the demand for cheap labor, the profitability of the triangle trade because of prevailing wind and ocean currents).

(Continued)

81

Figure 5.12 (Continued)

	Task	Objective	Knowledge Focus	Subject, Grade	Benchmark Statement
	energy of ambitious settlers from other lands, has grown to be a powerful and wealthy nation largely because of these resources. We've also seen that the history of the Athenians, whose sea power was unrivaled and unchecked, also supports the generalization that with great power can come great arrogance, and through arrogance, defeat. What does this suggest to you about the relationship of the past and present, whether the subject is geography or history? Provide evidence for your conclusions.				
Information: Organizing Principle	We've explored the ways in which music reflects different cultures and times. We've also discussed how, though cultures can last centuries, popular music seems to come and go fairly quickly. However, some songs that were popular in the early to mid-twentieth century are still heard today. Based on what you know about the songs that survive, what generalizations can you make about new music and whether it will stand the test of time?	The student will be able to provide generalizations on how the qualities of music help a particular piece of music endure.	Principles about the relationship between music and culture	Music 6–8	Understands characteristics of classic music and classic music genres as well as the factors affecting what makes music classic (e.g., from different genres, styles, historical periods, composers).

	Task	Objective	Knowledge Focus	Subject, Grade	Benchmark Statement
Mental Procedure: Skill	We have studied a number of refusal skills to be used in different situations. What generalization can you make about refusal skills regardless of the situations in which they are used?	The student will be able to construct a generalization about the use of specific refusal skills.	Specific refusal strategies	Health 6–8	Understand various refusal strategies and the situations in which they are best applied.
	We have studied various ways of recording time—the Egyptian and the Mayan, for example—and the systems on which they are based—for example, solar or lunar. What can we say is true about the technique that is used to record time, regardless of the system being used?	The student will be able to develop a generalization about the observational and data-gathering skills required to record time throughout history.	Observational and data-gathering skills	Historical Understanding 5–6	Understands various systems for recording time (e.g., Egyptian, Indian, Mayan, Muslim, Jewish) as well as the astronomical systems that are the foundation of such systems (e.g., solar, lunar, semilunar); evaluates their strengths and weaknesses.
Mental Procedure: Process	What generalizations about effective writing can be made when we consider what is required to write an effective essay, paragraph, or even an effective sentence?	The student will be able to generalize about the writing process required for the development of an effective sentence and its application to an effective essay or the reverse.	The writing process	Language Arts 9–12	Uses accurate and sensory language to clarify and enhance ideas and support various purposes (e.g., to tell an imaginative story, to translate complex concepts into simple terms, to achieve a specific voice, to defend literary concepts).
	How might you characterize innovation in a way that captures its uses and value in literature, the arts and technology?	The student will be able to create a generalization that captures the significant aspects of innovation across subject areas.	The process of invention	Technology 6–8	Understands the similarities and differences in the terms *invention* and *innovation* (e.g., invention is the process of creating a new system or object while innovation is the process of enhancing or adapting an existing system or object).

(Continued)

Figure 5.12 (Continued)

	Task	Objective	Knowledge Focus	Subject, Grade	Benchmark Statement
Psychomotor Procedure: Skill	What can be said generally about the motions common in gestures used by Italian speakers?	The student will be able to generalize about gestures that are common among speakers of the target language.	The skill of using gestures in a specific language.	Foreign Language 9–12	Knows about writing systems in the target and native languages as well as any other selected language (e.g., logographic, syllabic, alphabetic).
	Select three related weight-lifting skills, such as the front and rear squat and the dead lift, and determine what can be said generally about the proper execution of these skills.	The student will be able to generalize about proper form in weight lifting based on what is known about proper form in three related lifts.	Specific weight-lifting techniques	Physical Education 7–8	Knows how to train and condition for select physical activities.
Psychomotor Procedure: Process	What generalizations can be made about using exercise equipment as opposed to the sport that it mimics (e.g., bike machines vs. bikes; cross-country skiing vs. cross-country ski machines; treadmills vs. running)?	The student will be able to generalize about the relationship of movement forms in sports to the movement forms possible using machines that mimic those sports.	The general process of using exercise equipment for specific sports	Physical Education 7–8	Knows how to train and condition for select physical activities.
	Based upon your experience in oil or watercolor painting, what can be said about the things to watch out for when layering one color over another?	The student will be able to generalize about attention to sequence and layering common to the processes of oil and water color painting.	The process of layering colors	Visual Arts 9–12	Understands that the medium, technique, and processes one uses affect the ideas or information being communicated.

1. Following is a set of statements we have been studying about life on earth. What are some conclusions you might come to that are supported by these generalizations? Explain your reasoning.

   a. There have been profound changes in the climate over the earth.

   b. Coordination and integration of action are generally slower in plants than in animals.

   c. There is an increasing complexity of structure and function from lower to higher forms of life.

   d. All life comes from life and produces its own kind of living organism.

   e. Light is a limiting factor of life.

2. What general conclusion can you infer about batting, based on your understanding of the following skills?

   a. Hitting a curve ball

   b. Hitting a fast ball

   c. Hitting a knuckle ball

   d. Hitting a slider

Commonly, graphic organizers like those in Figure 5.13 are used as guides and aids in generalizing tasks.

The rows of the generalization matrix list the information from which a generalization is to be developed. In this case, the matrix addresses four types of

Figure 5.13   Generalizing Matrix

	Characteristic 1: Who Governs	Characteristic 2: How Decisions Are Made	Characteristic 3: Current Examples	Conclusions
Item 1: Democracy				
Item 2: Republic				
Item 3: Theocracy				
Item 4: Dictatorship				
Conclusions				

government: democracy, republic, theocracy, and dictatorship. The columns represent the specific characteristics that will be used to create the generalization. In this case, those characteristics are (a) who governs, (b) how decisions are made, and (c) current examples. Note that generalizations can be constructed for each type of government (row generalizations) and for each characteristic (column generalizations). The bottom right square in the matrix contains the summary generalization.

Generalizing With Information

As it relates to details, generalizing tasks involve inferring generalizations and principles from specific terms, facts, or events. For example, the first generalizing task for details involves facts about settlements from ancient times. Students must use their knowledge of details about ancient times to create new conclusions about settlements. Generalizing is a fairly sophisticated skill as it relates to organizing ideas. It involves the articulation of new generalizations and principles based on known generalizations and principles. For example, the first generalizing task for organizing ideas addresses a number of generalizations across the topics of history and geography. To complete this task, students must understand generalizations about history and geography and also make inferences to devise a larger overarching generalization.

Generalizing With Mental Procedures

Generalizing tasks for mental skills involve constructing and defending conclusions about a set of skills. For example, the first generalizing task for mental skills involves specific refusal skills. Students must use their understanding of specific refusal skills to create an overarching conclusion about refusal skills. Generalizing tasks for mental processes involve constructing and defending conclusions about two or more processes. For example, the first generalizing task for mental processes involves related processes for writing essays, paragraphs, and sentences. Students must create a generalization about writing that applies to these three situations.

Generalizing With Psychomotor Procedures

Generalizing tasks for psychomotor procedures follow the same pattern as for mental procedures. The first generalizing task for psychomotor skills involves constructing and defending generalizations about the skill of using gestures in Italian. The first generalizing task for psychomotor processes involves constructing and defending generalizations about processes for using exercise equipment for specific sports.

SPECIFYING

The analysis skill of specifying involves making and defending predictions about what might happen or what will necessarily happen in a given situation. Figure 5.14 lists specifying tasks and objectives across the domains of knowledge.

Specifying objectives and tasks can use the term *specify* along with terms and phrases like the following:

- Make and defend
- Predict
- Judge
- Deduce
- What would have to happen
- Develop an argument for
- Under what conditions

Specifying tasks typically use short and extended written or oral constructed-response formats.

Specifying With Information

As depicted in Figure 5.14, specifying does not apply well to details because details are inherently too specific to involve rules from which predictions can be made. On the other hand, specifying is a natural type of thinking relative to organizing ideas, which, by definition, are rule based. Specifying, as it relates to generalizations, involves identifying what might be or must be true about a specific item based on an understanding of the class or category to which that item belongs. For example, the first specifying task for organizing ideas uses generalizations regarding the right of habeas corpus to predict what must be true in a specific newspaper article. Specifying as it relates to principles involves making and defending predictions about what will or might happen under certain conditions. For example, the second specifying task for organizing ideas addresses principles regarding the change processes on earth. Based on these principles, students must conclude what must be true relative to a specific weather pattern.

Specifying With Mental Procedures

Specifying, as it relates to mental skills and processes, involves identifying what must happen or might happen during the execution of the skill or process under specific conditions. For example, the first specifying task for mental skills focuses on making predictions based on an understanding of the skills of reading

Figure 5.14 Specifying Objectives and Tasks

	Task	Objective	Knowledge Focus	Subject, Grade	Benchmark Statement
Information: Details: Terms, Facts, Time sequences	N/A				
	N/A				
Information: Organizing Generalization	If a newspaper editorial described an action as "dangerous to civil liberty," and said "that every defendant deserves to know of what he is charged," what topic in the Bill of Rights do you believe the editorial was concerned about? Explain why the newspaper article must be referring to the topic you have identified.	The student will be able to identify the circumstances that bear directly on the right of habeas corpus.	Generalizations regarding the right of habeas corpus.	Civics 6–8	Understands how the power of government is limited in order to protect the rights of individuals by specific provisions of the United States Constitution (including the Bill of Rights, e.g., habeas corpus; trial by jury; double jeopardy; ex post facto; freedom of religion, speech, press, and assembly; equal protection and due process of law; right to counsel).
Information: Organizing Principle	If a classmate argues that recent December snowstorms provide evidence that earth's climate is not changing, what principles would you argue are being assumed about the nature of climate change? What principles are being ignored?	The student will be able to identify circumstances that indicate fast processes of change on earth and those that indicate slower processes.	Principles regarding fast and slower processes of change on earth	Science 3–5	Understands how the earth's surface is constantly changing by both slow and rapid processes (e.g., slow processes, such as weathering, erosion, transport, and deposition of sediment caused by waves, wind, water, and ice; rapid processes, such as tornadoes, volcanic eruptions, and earthquakes).

	Task	Objective	Knowledge Focus	Subject, Grade	Benchmark Statement
Mental Procedure: Skill	We have been studying various map projections and how different projections distort the relationship of land masses in different ways. If you compared Greenland and Africa by estimating their square miles using a Mercator map and then compared them using a globe, how would the comparisons differ and why?	The student will be able to make and defend inferences about map reading based on an understanding of the effects of different map projections.	The skills of reading a Mercator map and a globe	Geography 6–8	Identifies the characteristics of map projections, such as distortion on a flat map projection and understands the purposes and best use of each type.
	If you change the dimensions of a square but keep it as a rectangle with the same unit area, how will its perimeter change?	The student will be able to make and defend inferences about the results of measuring, based on an understanding of the relationship between perimeter and area.	The skill of measuring length, perimeter, and area	Math 3–5	Understands relationships between length, perimeter, circumference, and area.
Mental Procedure: Process	You've written an expository essay on the victims of a recent hurricane. When you finished, you decided you should persuade your classmates to help you raise money for the cause. How would your writing and approach change, and what would you keep? Explain how your changes would improve the chances of persuading your classmates.	The student will be able to make and defend an inference about the development of a persuasive essay based on an understanding of the relationship of persuasive writing to other types of writing.	The process of writing a persuasive essay	Language Arts 6–8	Writes persuasive compositions (e.g., engages the reader by using context and persona; develops a master idea that conveys an opinion; creates and organizes an appropriate structure for a specific audience; includes details, reasons, and examples persuasively; excludes irrelevant information; anticipates and addresses counter claims; cites sources of information as appropriate).

(Continued)

Figure 5.14 (Continued)

	Task	Objective	Knowledge Focus	Subject, Grade	Benchmark Statement
	If you set up an investigation that assumed constant temperature for both experimental and control conditions, under what conditions and how might you salvage your experiment, if the temperature was found not to be constant?	The student will be able to make and defend an inference about the interpretation of an investigation and the evaluation of an explanation by carefully accounting for all variations and determining their relevance to the stated purpose.	The mental process of conducting an investigation	Science 9–12	Knows that concepts and knowledge guide all scientific inquiries, while current scientific discovery influences the design and interpretation of investigations and evaluations made by other scientists.
Psychomotor Procedure: Skill	Given what you know about vocalizing and voice projection, what would likely be the result if you vocalized from your throat rather than from your diaphragm?	The student will be able to make and defend an inference about the effects of different types of vocalization based on an understanding of the mechanics of the skill.	The skill of vocalizing	Theatre 9–12	Understands both contemporary and classic acting technique.
	The cue-ball and eight-ball are in a direct line to the corner pocket. What would likely happen if you sank the eight-ball using bottom English on the cue ball?	The student will be able to make and defend an inference regarding the effect of different types of English on the cue ball, based on an understanding of cue ball control.	The skill of putting English on a cue ball	Physical Education 7–8	Understands sophistication in movement associated with highly skilled athletes (e.g., what makes successful serves, passes, and spikes in volleyball).
Psychomotor Procedure: Process	If you consistently rush the net after you deliver every serve, what would your opponent likely do in response?	The student will be able to make and defend an inference on the likely strategy of an opponent, if the opponent is presented with consistent behavior.	The process of playing tennis	Physical Education 9–12	Knows and follows the rules for sporting activities and uses appropriate offensive and defensive strategies.
	If you begin a musical piece at the wrong tempo, what impact might this have on musical phrases within the piece and for the impression of the piece overall?	The student will be able to make and defend inferences about the impact of a given tempo on various aspects of a musical performance.	The process of performing a musical piece	Music 6–8	Accurately performs on a classroom instrument a variety of pieces that display modest ranges and changes of tempo, key, and meter.

a Mercator map and reading a globe. The first specifying task for mental processes focuses on making predictions based on an understanding of the process of writing a persuasive essay.

Specifying With Psychomotor Procedures

Specifying tasks for psychomotor procedures are the same as specifying tasks for mental procedures—students identify what must happen or might happen in the execution of a procedure under certain conditions. For example, the first specifying task for psychomotor skills focuses on making predictions based on an understanding of the skill of vocalizing. The first specifying task for psychomotor processes focuses on making predictions based on an understanding of the process of playing tennis.

SUMMARY OF KEY POINTS FOR ANALYSIS OBJECTIVES AND TASKS

Matching Objectives and Tasks

- Require students to identify similarities and differences
- Use terms and phrases like the following: match, categorize, compare, compare and contrast, differentiate, discriminate, distinguish, sort, create an analogy, create a metaphor
- Use short or extended written and oral constructed-response formats
- Use specific types of graphic organizers

Classifying Objectives and Tasks

- Require students to identify superordinate and subordinate categories
- Use terms and phrases like the following: classify, organize, sort, identify a broader category, identify categories, identify different types
- Use short or extended written and oral constructed-response formats
- Use specific types of graphic organizers

Analyzing Errors Objectives and Tasks

- Require students to identify logical errors in information and processing errors in the execution of procedural knowledge
- Use terms and phrases like the following: analyze the errors in, identify problems, identify issues, identify misunderstandings, assess, critique, diagnose, evaluate, edit, revise
- Use short or extended written and oral constructed-response formats

Generalizing Objectives and Tasks

- Require students to infer new generalizations and principles from known information
- Use terms and phrases like the following: generalize, what conclusions can be drawn, what references can be made, create a generalization, create a principle, create a rule, trace the development, form conclusions
- Use short or extended written and oral constructed-response formats
- Use specific types of graphic organizers

Specifying Objectives and Tasks

- Require students to make and defend predictions about what might happen or what will necessarily happen in a given situation
- Use terms and phrases like the following: make and defend, specify, predict, judge, deduce, what would have to happen, develop an argument for, under what conditions
- Use short or extended written or oral constructed-response formats

CHAPTER SIX

Knowledge Utilization Objectives and Tasks

The knowledge utilization processes require students to apply or use knowledge in specific situations. There are four knowledge utilization processes: (1) decision making, (2) problem solving, (3) experimenting, and (4) investigating. We consider each.

DECISION MAKING

Decision making involves selecting among alternatives that initially appear equal. Figure 6.1 lists decision-making objectives and tasks for the various domains of knowledge.

The term *decide* is commonly used in decision-making objectives and tasks along with other terms and phrases including the following:

- Select the best among the following alternatives
- Which among the following would be the best
- What is the best way
- Which of these is most suitable

The most common format for decision-making tasks is short or extended written or oral constructed-response formats. Sometimes decision-making tasks are quite structured, as in the following example:

Assume that the following three sites are being considered as the location for a new waste disposal plant: (1) near the lake at the north end of town, (2) near the airport, and (3) in the mountains outside of town. Which site would be best? Explain why the specific characteristics of the site you selected make it the best selection.

(*Text continues on page 98*)

Figure 6.1 Decision-Making Objectives and Tasks

	Task	Objective	Knowledge Focus	Subject, Grade	Benchmark Statement
Information: Details: Terms, Facts, Time sequences	Using the data you have from your most recent fitness assessment, decide what aspects of your personal fitness need attention and what you might do to improve your overall fitness.	The student will be able to use data from a personal fitness assessment and knowledge about fitness components to make a decision about how to improve overall fitness.	Details from a personal fitness report	Physical Education 3–6	Improves select fitness components through attention to relevant assessments (e.g., cardio-respiratory endurance, muscular strength and endurance, flexibility, and body composition).
	We've been learning that rules might be useful in one situation but not in another. Use our four rules for classroom behavior and decide which of the following three situations would benefit most if it used our rules: your home, people traveling together on a vacation, politicians in the government.	The student will be able to decide which nonschool situations would benefit from established school rules.	Details about specific behavioral rules	Behavioral Studies 3–5	Understands that even consistent rules, such as the ones at home, school, church and in the community, are subject to change (e.g., some rules become outdated, new people are involved, outside circumstances change).
Information: Organizing Generalization	You are helping design the stage for a school production for a play set in 1890s Denver. Based on what you know about this time in the West, decide what kinds of props and scenery will likely be part of every outdoor street scene.	The student will be able to decide on the props and scenery needed for a play set in the American West, based on an understanding of how to create an environment on stage and knowledge of some aspects of the American West.	Generalizations about props and scenery	Theater 5–8	Creates environments through scenery, properties, lighting and sound choices and characters through costume and makeup choices.

	Task	Objective	Knowledge Focus	Subject, Grade	Benchmark Statement
Information: Organizing Principle	You have team sprints scheduled for this afternoon. You've got a snack high in carbohydrates, a candy bar that's high in sugar and fat, and a protein drink. Based on what you know about principles of nutrition and the impact of physical activities, which should you choose before your exercise?	The student will be able to decide what food choices are the most beneficial, based on an understanding of nutrition and the demands of either aerobic or anaerobic activities.	Principles of nutrition	Health 9–12	Understands how people of different genders, ages, and activity levels have different nutrient and energy needs.
Mental Procedure: Skill	You were given four three-digit numbers—362, 459, 921, and 658—and asked to quickly estimate the sum in your head. Identify at least two ways of doing this and then explain which would be the best way to do so. Consider speed and accuracy in your decision.	The student will be able to decide, based on a familiarity with estimation strategies, which strategies are appropriate for a particular problem type.	Estimation skills and strategies	Math 3–5	Uses strategies (e.g., front-end estimation, rounding) to estimate computations and to evaluate those estimations.
	You've just discovered that the data you imported into a spreadsheet has a significant flaw: All the data have been shifted by one column, so that the variable names identify the wrong data. Determine how you will restore or reimport the data and explain your reasoning. Consider at least two methods for accomplishing this task and at least two criteria by which you will make your decision.	The student will be able to decide, based on an understanding of the process of importing data, what approach is most efficient for correcting import errors.	Data-manipulation strategies	Technology 9–12	Imports, exports, and merges data stored in different formats (e.g., text, graphics).

(Continued)

Figure 6.1 (Continued)

	Task	Objective	Knowledge Focus	Subject, Grade	Benchmark Statement
Mental Procedure: Process	You've been asked to write a letter to persuade a city council person to visit your civics class and describe the job's duties and responsibilities. What strategies would you use to make the invitation an appealing one? Consider at least three strategies we have studied, such as appeal to emotion, appeal to reason, and appeal to tradition.	The student will be able to decide how to employ persuasive writing strategies that are most effective for a particular audience and purpose.	Processes for persuasive writing	Language Arts 9–12	Adapts writing for different purposes (e.g., to inform, analyze, entertain, persuade).
	We have been studying ways to learn and remember new information. Three of these ways are (a) verbatim rehearsal, (b) mnemonic devices, and (c) extended practice. Select something you would like to learn and decide which of these three approaches would be best, given the content you have selected. Use at least two criteria while making your decision.	The student will be able to decide, based on an understanding of learning strategies, the best way to learn new personally chosen content.	The process of learning new knowledge	Health 9–12	Knows and applies a number of strategies for learning new knowledge.
Psychomotor Procedure: Skill	You've always played tennis on asphalt courts, and today you'll be playing a match on a grass court for the first time. Consider at least three strategies for hitting a forehand groundstroke. Which of them would most likely be the best approach to use and why? Describe the criteria you used to make your decision.	The student will be able to decide, based on an understanding of the way that different surfaces affect travel in tennis, how best to return a forehand on a different surface.	Strategies for hitting a forehand stroke	Physical Education 7–8	Understands sophistication in movement associated with highly skilled athletes.

	Task	Objective	Knowledge Focus	Subject, Grade	Benchmark Statement
	You've been asked to create a dance sequence that makes people think of a specific animal. Which of the dance movements we have been practicing would you use? Why?	The student will be able to decide, based on an understanding of dance, what movements to use for a dance with a specific purpose.	Specific dance movements	Dance K–4	Creates a sequence of movements with a specific impression in mind.
Psychomotor Procedure: Process	The scene you will play requires that, by the end of the scene, you transform from a quiet and reserved character to someone bold and confident. Decide how you will transform yourself over the course of the scene so that the transition is believable. Identify specific physical actions you might use and prioritize them in terms of their utility. Explain the criteria you used to prioritize the strategy.	The student will be able to decide, based on an understanding of the acting process, how best to communicate a significant change in a character over time that also maintains credibility with the audience.	Physical strategies used in the acting process	Theater 9–12	Creates and maintains believable characters that communicate with audiences in improvisations and productions.
	You'd like to create an oil painting that evokes in the viewer an immediate sense of the surface texture or even a three-dimensional, sculptural feel. Decide what techniques and processes you would use and why you believe they will be effective. Identify the strategies you might consider and the criteria you used to select your strategies.	The student will be able to decide, based on an understanding of painting techniques, how to create a specific visual effect.	Strategies within the process of painting	Visual Arts 9–12	Understands how the media and processes one uses affect the communication of ideas.

Here the alternatives are provided to students. This is in contrast to a task like the following, which requires students to generate the alternatives:

What site would be the best location for a waste-disposal plant? Identify at least three viable potential sites and explain why the specific characteristics of the site you selected make it the best selection.

When decision-making tasks are highly structured, it is common to provide students with a decision-making matrix like that shown in Figure 6.2.

The matrix in Figure 6.2 is set up for the decision-making task about the best site for a waste-disposal park. The alternatives form the columns. The criteria that will be used to select among the alternatives form the rows. In the task, three alternatives are being considered: (1) near the lake at the north end of town, (2) near the airport, and (3) in the mountains outside of town. Also three criteria are being used: (A) moderate to low cost, (B) environmentally safe, and (C) aesthetically pleasing. A "Y" indicates that an alternative meets a criterion. For example, the first alternative (near the lake) meets the first criterion (moderate to low cost). An "N" indicates that an alternative does not meet the criterion, and a "?" indicates that the student is not sure whether the alternative meets the criterion. Once the matrix is completed, the student looks at the pattern of "Y" responses to determine the best alternative. In this case, it is the first alternative, near the lake. For a discussion of more sophisticated types of decision-making matrices, see Marzano (2007).

We next consider decision-making tasks across the various domains of knowledge.

Decision Making With Information

Details are frequently the criteria used in decisions. For example, the first decision-making task for details requires students to use details from a personal

Figure 6.2   Decision-Making Matrix

	Alternative 1 Near the Lake	Alternative 2 Near the Airport	Alternative 3 In the Mountains Outside of Town
Criterion 1: Moderate to low cost	Y	Y	?
Criterion 2: Environmentally safe	Y	N	?
Criterion 3: Aesthetically pleasing	Y	N	Y

fitness report to make a decision about how to improve overall fitness. Organizing ideas are also common criteria used to make selections between alternatives. For example, the first decision-making task for organizing ideas requires students to use generalizations about props and scenery to determine how best to create a specific environment on stage.

Decision Making With Mental Procedures

Mental skills are sometimes used as explicit tools with which to gather information for decisions. For example, the first decision-making task for mental *skills* requires students to use their knowledge of estimation skills to decide on the best approach to solve a specific type of problem. The second decision-making task for mental *processes* requires students to use their knowledge of learning strategies to determine the best approach to learn new content of their choice.

Decision Making With Psychomotor Procedures

Psychomotor skills and processes can also be used when making decisions. For example, the second decision-making task for psychomotor skills requires students to use their knowledge of specific dance movements to determine the best way to convey a specific impression. The first decision-making task for psychomotor processes requires students to use their knowledge of physical strategies in acting to determine the best way to convey a specific impression on stage.

PROBLEM SOLVING

The knowledge utilization process of problem solving involves accomplishing a goal for which obstacles or limiting conditions exist. Problem solving is closely related to decision making in that the latter is frequently a subcomponent of problem solving. However, whereas decision making does not involve obstacles to a goal, problem solving does. Figure 6.3 lists sample problem-solving objectives and tasks across the knowledge domains.

The term *solve* is frequently used in problem-solving tasks and objectives along with terms and phrases like the following:

- How would you overcome
- Adapt
- Develop a strategy to
- Figure out a way to
- How will you reach your goal under these conditions

The most common format for problem-solving tasks is short or extended written and constructed-response formats.

(*Text continues on page 104*)

Figure 6.3 Problem-Solving Objectives and Tasks

	Task	Objective	Knowledge Focus	Subject, Grade	Benchmark Statement
Information: Details: Terms, Facts, Time sequences	We have been studying the proposed wind farm on the north side of town. All sources of energy, including alternative energy sources, present problems, such as unevenness of supply, and trade-offs, such as less expense at the cost of convenience. Identify the current greatest obstacles—social, physical, technical, or a combination of these—and the solutions needed for the adoption of the proposed project.	The student will be able to propose a solution for the adoption of specific alternative energy sources based on an understanding of the obstacles and trade-offs associated with its use.	Details about a specific alternative energy source	Geography 9–12	Understands how the widespread use of renewable energy sources (e.g., solar, wind, thermal) might affect both the earth and society (e.g., air and water quality, the oil industries, and current manufacturing practices).
	We have seen an endorsement from a television celebrity regarding the positive effects of new exercise equipment for flattening your stomach; however, neither the commercial nor the company that has provided any evidence of its effectiveness. How will you overcome this problem? Where will you go to find the necessary information?	The student will be able to identify alternative sources of health-related information when none appear available.	Details about a specific type of exercise equipment	Health 9–12	Knows how to determine whether various resources from home, school, and the community present valid health information, products, and services.
Information: Organizing Generalization	Poor nations may believe that they do not have strong enough voices at the U.N., but wealthy nations, who significantly impact trade and commerce in the world, likely believe that this strength of their influence should reflect this greater contribution. How might the structure of the U.N. be revised to accommodate both concerns? To solve this problem, use what you know of the ideas developed and agreements forged during the Constitutional Convention.	The student will be able to propose a solution to a problem regarding political representation based on an understanding of issues raised during the Constitutional Convention and how they were resolved.	Generalizations proposed during the Constitutional Convention	U.S. History 5–6	Knows the important issues of the time of the Constitutional Convention and which of them were supported and which were opposed (e.g., separation of powers, checks and balances, the Virginia Plan, the New Jersey Plan, the Connecticut Compromise, abolition).

	Task	Objective	Knowledge Focus	Subject, Grade	Benchmark Statement
Information: Organizing Principles	Based on what you have learned about an ecosystem, including such principles as predator–prey relationships, competition for resources, and the acceptable range of temperatures for certain species, develop a terrarium that you believe provides its inhabitants with the strongest possibility of a long life. Identify the significant problems you faced in selection of species and the environment and how you solved them.	The student will be able to address the problems that threaten survival of a selected species based on an understanding of predator–prey relationships, competition for resources, and requirements for food and a supporting environment.	Principles regarding ecosystems	Science 6–8	Knows factors that affect the number and types of organisms an ecosystem can support (e.g., available resources; abiotic factors, such as quantity of light and water, range of temperatures, and soil composition; disease; competition from other organisms within the ecosystem; predation).
Mental Procedure: Skill	We've been studying various kinds of refusal skills. If you had a friend who recognized that others were making him act in a way that might harm his health but who was unable to resist their influence, what advice or strategy would you offer and why?	The student will be able to identify how best to solve a problem of negative social influence through understanding the best use of refusal skills.	Specific refusal skills	Health 3–5	Understands techniques for avoiding, and responding to, negative social influences and pressure to use alcohol or drugs (e.g., refusal skills, self-control).
	While scanning a topographic map for information about a specific mountain, you see that the contour line for the ridge you are interested in does not have a number associated with it, although there are contour lines near it that do have altitudes assigned. Describe how you will determine the altitude of the contour line and how you will determine whether it is in feet or meters.	The student will be able to solve the problem of missing information on a map through the use of basic map-reading skills.	Reading a contour map	Geography 3–5	Identifies the basic characteristics of maps and globes (e.g., title, legend, cardinal and intermediate directions, scale, grid, principal parallels, meridians, projection).

(Continued)

Figure 6.3 (Continued)

	Task	Objective	Knowledge Focus	Subject, Grade	Benchmark Statement
Mental Procedure: Process	While working on a research paper, you discover conflicting claims among the sources you use regarding a specific, critical event. How will you resolve the problem? Discuss the processes available, including evaluating the credibility of sources, verifying the facts, and determining whether logical inferences are made from facts.	The student will be able to resolve a question of conflicting information through evaluating the credibility of sources, verifying facts, and evaluating inferences made from facts.	The process of finding, citing, and using sources in a research paper	Language Arts 9–12	Writes research papers (e.g., uses a thesis statement, uses an appropriate organization pattern, paraphrases ideas and connects them to sources, identifies nuances and discrepancies in information, addresses all possible perspectives, uses visual aids when necessary, integrates quotations and citations correctly, adapts researched material for presentation in anticipation of a particular audience).
	You are tasked with writing an essay that will persuade both your peers and parents in the community to contribute money toward the building of a high-tech classroom that won't be completed until after you graduate. How will you craft arguments that will persuade both audiences to contribute to the cause?	The student will be able to solve the problem of appealing to different audiences in the same essay by using a variety of persuasive techniques.	The process of writing a persuasive essay	Language Arts 9–12	Writes persuasive compositions that address problems–solutions or causes–effects (e.g., uses a thesis statement; addresses all possible counter arguments; uses rhetorical devices, such as appeals to logic and appeals to emotion; uses personal anecdotes; develops arguments and uses details, addresses tradition, cause-and-effect reasoning, comparison–contrast reasoning).

	Task	Objective	Knowledge Focus	Subject, Grade	Benchmark Statement
Psychomotor Procedure: Skill	The fingering supplied for an instrumental piece you are studying does not work for the size and shape of your hands. Based on what works best for you, assign new fingering wherever needed.	The student will be able to solve a specific fingering problem by revising fingering notation to best meet personal skills and limitations.	Fingering skills for a specific instrument	Music 6–8	Accurately performs a variety of instrumental pieces with expression on a classroom instrument, demonstrating mastery of modest ranges and changes of tempo, key, and meter.
	You are to present a speech in the foreign language we are studying, and you have had consistent problems pronouncing some of the words in the speech. How might you write out the speech for yourself to ensure that you say each word correctly?	The student will be able to solve a problem of pronunciation through making notes to self in an unfamiliar language about correct pronunciation.	Correct pronunciation in a foreign language	Foreign Language K–4	Presents simple oral reports about common school and home activities.
Psychomotor Procedure: Process	Because of a recent injury, you find that your backhand is not as strong as it should be. Devise a method of play that will capitalize on your other strengths to offset this problem.	The student will be able to solve a specific sports-skill problem by identifying strategies that will compensate.	Playing tennis	Physical Education 9–12	Follows the rules of a selected sport and makes use of offensive and defensive techniques.
	The character you've been selected to play is very old, which you won't be for a long time. Describe what physical techniques you'll use to make the audience believe that you are much older than you appear.	The student will be able to solve acting challenges through an understanding of techniques used to project characters of a specific type.	The process of portraying a character	Theatre 9–12	Understands various classical and contemporary acting techniques and methods.

Problem Solving With Information

Details are frequently used to solve problems. For example, the first problem-solving task for details requires an understanding of details about a specific alternative energy source. Organizing ideas apply to a variety of problem-solving tasks. Commonly, a student uses a generalization or principle when identifying how best to overcome the obstacle within the problem. For example, the first problem-solving task for organizing ideas involves the use of generalizations proposed at the Constitutional Convention to help solve a hypothetical problem about the United Nations.

Problem Solving With Mental Procedures

Specific mental skills can be the subject of problem-solving tasks. For example, the first problem-solving task for mental skills involves refusal skills. In this task, effective use of refusal skills is the vehicle used to solve the problem. In the second example, the problem exists within the execution of the mental process itself: There is an obstacle to the typical procedure for reading a contour map—altitudes are not assigned to the contour lines. Mental processes are commonly the subject of problem solving. The first problem-solving task for mental processes involves the process of finding, citing and using sources in research papers. In this case, the obstacle is that this process has produced conflicting results.

Problem Solving With Psychomotor Procedures

The first example of a problem-solving task for psychomotor skills involves fingering skills for a specific instrument. The constraint is that a new system of fingering must be designed by students. The first example of a problem-solving task for psychomotor processes involves the process of playing tennis. The obstacle in this situation is that an injury has limited the use of the student's backhand stroke.

EXPERIMENTING

Experimenting involves generating and testing hypotheses about a specific physical or psychological phenomenon. A critical feature of experimenting tasks is that the data be newly collected by the student. Figure 6.4 lists experimenting objectives and tasks across the various domains of knowledge.

The terms *generate* and *test* are commonly used in experimenting objectives and tasks, along with terms and phrases like the following:

- Generate and test
- Test the idea that

(*Text continues on page 109*)

Figure 6.4 Experimenting Objectives and Tasks

	Task	Objective	Knowledge Focus	Subject, Grade	Benchmark Statement
Information: Details: Terms, Facts, Time sequences	Identify a recent significant event and hypothesize how different types of people in the community will view it. Provide the reasoning for your hypothesis and then survey members of the community to test your hypothesis.	The student will be able to generate and test a hypothesis about how selected events might be viewed by different members of the community.	Details about a specific current event	Health 9–12	Understands that events can be viewed differently by different types of people.
	Select a development in technology that has occurred in the past twenty years. For example, you might select the iPod. Based on what we have discussed about how such changes impact society, develop a hypothesis about how that technology has had an impact on people's lives. Then gather information that will directly test your hypothesis.	The student will be able to generate and test a hypothesis that demonstrates an understanding of the possible impact of a recent technology on society.	Details about a specific technological innovation	Technology 6–8	Understands how technology and society affect one another (e.g., new technologies are developed to serve the process and product needs of society; as society, economy, and politics change, so does technology; societal needs, values, and beliefs influence technology).
Information: Organizing Generalization	We know that there are good reasons for people choosing one kind of geography over another when choosing a place to live. For example, in agricultural and early societies, settling near fertile soil was critical for survival, not simply convenient for livelihood. Based on how we live now, develop a hypothesis about what essential aspects people look for when they consider moving to a new place. Why might the reasons be different? How can you collect information directly from people to answer this question?	The student will be able to generate and test a hypothesis regarding the reasons why people choose to live in certain places.	Generalizations about why humans establish settlements	Geography 3–5	Identifies areas of dense human population and understands reasons for such population (e.g., fertile soil, availability of water; availability of coal, iron, and other natural resources).

(Continued)

105

Figure 6.4 (Continued)

	Task	Objective	Knowledge Focus	Subject, Grade	Benchmark Statement
Information: Organizing Principle	Select three different visual structures that, according to the design principles we've been studying, can have different effects on the viewer, such as a sense of balance, anxiety, or rhythm. Create simple drawings that you believe exemplify each structure and find out if you are successful in communicating what you intend. For example, survey your classmates to tell you which drawing represents which effect. Decide if, based on the results, you can change the design to improve your results.	The student will be able to generate and test a hypothesis regarding design principles and their effects on the viewer.	Principles of design in art	Visual Arts 5–8	Understands how different physical structures produce certain effects (e.g., design elements, such as line, color, shape; principles such as repetition, rhythm, balance).
Mental Procedure: Skill	Imagine a scenario in which you have a limited amount of money and are in the grocery store adding items to a shopping cart. You don't have a calculator, so you've got to keep a running total in your head of the costs of the items as you add them. Develop two or more techniques for mentally estimating or calculating the totals as you go. You can even develop techniques that use items in your cart to help you keep some track of your running total. How would you go about testing the effectiveness of your approaches?	The student will be able to generate a hypothesis regarding the best math strategies to use to solve a specific estimation problem and test their relative effectiveness.	Strategies for solving a specific type of mathematics problem	Math 6–8	Understands that different techniques (e.g., working backward from a solution, using a similar problem type, identifying a pattern) may be used to solve the same mathematical problem but that some of those techniques may be more effective for that particular problem than others.
	Using time as a measure is very useful in science as in daily life. We can compare the speed of two things, like marbles moving down an inclined plane, because we can say how much time each takes to travel the same distance. But watches aren't the only way that we can measure time. We can also use water: If we can make it flow at a steady rate, it allows us to make comparisons. Create a hypothesis about how the flow of water can be controlled so that it can be used to measure time. How can you test it?	The student will be able to generate a hypothesis about how water might be used to keep track of time and then test the hypothesis by constructing the device.	Skills and strategies for measuring time	Science 3–5	Uses simple tools and equipment (e.g., thermometers, microscopes, calculators, graduated cylinders) to collect scientific data.

	Task	Objective	Knowledge Focus	Subject, Grade	Benchmark Statement
Mental Procedure: Process	We have been studying how to use various search engines. Generate a hypothesis about the most efficient and most accurate research engine for a specific type of information. Then test your hypothesis and explain your findings.	The student will be able to generate and test a hypothesis about the use of various search engines.	Strategies for using a variety of search engines	Technology 6–8	Understands the uses of a variety of informational search engines.
	We've been studying various map projections. Based on what you've learned, hypothesize about what characteristic of a map projection would provide you the greatest likelihood of getting the most accurate distance measurement between two points at some fixed point on the earth. What projection would be least likely to provide accurate information for the same locations? Determine whether you are correct by comparing the known distance between the two points against the distance you determine through the map projections.	The student will be able to generate a hypothesis about which map projection will provide more and less accurate data about the distance between two places and test that hypothesis through measurement.	Strategies for using a variety of maps	Geography 6–8	Knows distinguishing characteristics of map projections, including distortion on flat-map projections, and identifies situations in which each map might be more or less beneficial.
Psychomotor Procedure: Skill	The Qwerty keyboard was designed to slow down typists because early mechanical typewriters were not well-designed and would jam easily. Computer keyboards don't jam, though, and August Dvorak designed a keyboard to make typing more comfortable and a little faster. Compare the two keyboard designs and generate a hypothesis that tests the usefulness of his design.	The student will be able to generate and test a hypothesis about the likely usefulness of a specific keyboarding invention in a specific situation.	Keyboarding	Technology 6–8	Types with some sophistication, demonstrating some memorization of key location.

(Continued)

Figure 6.4 (Continued)

	Task	Objective	Knowledge Focus	Subject, Grade	Benchmark Statement
	We have been studying a number of stretching techniques. Generate and test a hypothesis about the effectiveness of a particular technique in a particular situation.	The student will be able to generate a hypothesis about the usefulness of a specific stretching technique.	Specific stretching techniques	Physical Education 6–8	Understands and applies stretching techniques in appropriate situations.
Psychomotor Procedure: Process	Keep a log of your exercise. Note the time of day, how long before and after a meal, the type of meal, how effective the exercise seemed to be, and whatever other information you think might be helpful. At the end of a three-week period, review the data to generate a hypothesis about the best conditions for exercise. Implement an exercise plan based on your hypotheses. After three weeks of your new plan, compare your before and after logs.	The student will be able to generate and test a hypothesis regarding the conditions that are optimal for personal exercise.	Personal exercise techniques	Health 9–12	Understands how personal habits relate to general health and how these habits can be modified if necessary to promote attainment of health goals (e.g., following a personal nutrition plan to reduce the risk of high blood pressure or cholesterol levels as well as disease).
	Select music from two different genres or styles. Identify what you think is most distinctive about each style so that you can select and play just a few measures that you think capture the differences. Ask your classmates to guess the style of each. Have you been able to capture the style?	The student will be able to generate a hypothesis about the characteristics of a musical style and check that hypothesis through a survey of listeners.	Performance techniques	Music 3–5	Demonstrates knowledge of music representing diverse genres and styles.

- What would happen if
- How would you test that
- How would you determine if
- How can this be explained
- Based on the experiment, what can be predicted

The most common formats for experimenting tasks are short and extended written and oral constructed-response tasks.

Experimenting With Information

Details are sometimes used as the basis for hypothesis generation and testing. For example, the first experimenting task for details involves details about a specific current event. Students must generate a hypothesis about how different people might perceive this event and then gather data to test their hypothesis. Experimenting is particularly well suited to organizing ideas since these knowledge structures readily lend themselves to hypothesis generation. For example, the first experimenting task for organizing ideas involves generalizations about why people choose to live in certain places. Students must generate hypotheses and then collect data to test these hypotheses.

Experimenting With Mental Procedures

Mental skills and processes can be used as the subject of experimenting tasks. For example, the first experimenting task for mental skills involves strategies for solving a specific type of problem. Students must generate and test hypotheses about the most efficient strategies for solving that particular problem type. The first experimenting task for mental processes involves strategies for using a variety of search engines. Students design an experiment to determine the most efficient search engine in a specific situation.

Experimenting With Psychomotor Procedures

Experimenting tasks for psychomotor skills and processes follow the same pattern as experimenting tasks for mental procedures. The first experimenting task for psychomotor skills involves generating and testing hypotheses for two keyboarding configurations. The first experimenting task for psychomotor processes involves generating and testing hypotheses regarding a personal exercise routine.

INVESTIGATING

Investigating involves examining a past, present, or future situation. Investigating can be likened to experimenting in that it involves hypothesis generation and testing.

However, the data used in investigating are not gathered by direct observation as they are in experimenting. Rather, the data used to test hypotheses are assertions and opinions that have been made by others. In addition, the rules of evidence for investigating tasks are different from those employed in experimenting inquiry. The rules of evidence for investigating are those governing the design of a logical argument. The rules of evidence for experimenting are those governing the interpretation of direct observations. Investigating may be likened more to investigative reporting, whereas experimenting may be likened more to pure scientific inquiry. Figure 6.5 lists investigating objectives and tasks across the domains of knowledge.

The term *investigate* can be used in investigating tasks along with terms and phrases like the following:

- Research
- Find out about
- Take a position on
- What are the differing features of
- How did this happen
- Why did this happen
- What would have happened if

The most common format for investigating tasks is short or extended oral and written constructed-response tasks.

Investigating With Information

Knowledge of specific details and organizing ideas are commonly the impetus for an investigation. For example, the first investigating task for details involves facts about obtaining food during a specific period of time. To complete the task, students must examine what others have said about the issue. The first investigating task for organizing ideas involves generalizations about people imitating characters in the media. Students are instructed to examine what others have said about this issue using information from the Internet along with other sources.

Investigating With Mental Procedures

Mental skills and processes are frequently the subject of investigating tasks. For example, the first investigating task for mental skills focuses on discovering the origins of base 10 computational algorithms. The first investigating task involving mental processes addresses the process of using Internet databases. Students must examine early origins of such databases.

(*Text continues on page 115*)

Figure 6.5   Investigating Objectives and Tasks

	Task	Objective	Knowledge Focus	Subject, Grade	Benchmark Statement
Information: Details: Terms, Facts, Time sequences	Select three kinds of basic foods that you eat every day, like bread, milk, and vegetables. How did a family in early America obtain the same kinds of food? Did this change how they spent their time?	The student will be able to investigate how acquiring daily food placed great demands on families of 1800s.	Details about families of the 1800s	History 3–4	Knows how a farm family from the early 1800s experienced daily life (e.g., work, clothing, tools, food, and food production).
	We've been studying how human actions can impact the environment. In 1972, 2 million old tires were dropped a mile off the coast of Florida, in a move thought to beneficial. Now there is a significant effort under way to remove all the tires at considerable expense. Determine why the plan was adopted originally, why the tires must now be removed, and, with the benefit of hindsight, what should have been investigated before the initial decision was made.	The student will be able to investigate how specific human decisions can significantly impact the environment.	Details about a specific human decision	Geography 9–12	Knows how the physical environment is affected by changes in human technology or behavior (e.g., runoff and sediment changes, soil and air quality degradation, habitat destruction, alterations in the hydrologic cycle, increases in world temperatures).
Information: Organizing Generalization	We know that people learn about others in many different ways, including talking with others and from mass media, like television and radio. Is it true that people sometimes imitate people or characters they see in television or the movies? Using the Internet and other sources, find out what others have said and written about this issue.	The student will be able to investigate the impact that television characters can have on individuals.	Generalizations about people imitating characters in the media	Behavioral Studies 3–5	Knows that characters seen in the media are sometimes imitated.

(Continued)

Figure 6.5 (Continued)

	Task	Objective	Knowledge Focus	Subject, Grade	Benchmark Statement
Information: Organizing Principle	We know that the source language for an English word or phrase is often associated with some topics but not others. For example, in medicine we find many terms or phrases that have their origin in Latin or Greek. Words that name farm animals tend to be from Old English or Anglo-Saxon—cow, deer, sheep—but the names for the meat from these animals often have a French origin—beef, venison, mutton. Explore families of words to determine if you can find any other relationships or associations. Come up with evidence for your word family and suggest a reason that the words share a common source language.	The student will be able to investigate word origins to identify principles or commonalities in word families.	Principles regarding word origins	Language Arts 6–8	Understands the meaning of unfamiliar words by using word origins and derivations (e.g., Latin and Greek roots, meanings of foreign words used in English, historical and contemporary influences on word meanings).
Mental Procedure: Skill	We have been studying different bases in mathematics. Of course, base 10 is the one we use. Using the Internet and other sources, describe the early origins of base 10 mathematics.	The student will be able to investigate the origins of base 10 mathematics.	Computational algorithms in the base 10 system	Math 6–8	Knows how number systems with bases other than 10 are structured (e.g., base 60 for telling time and measuring angles, Roman numerals for dates and clock faces).
	In the past, people used different tools to measure weight. Ask your parents and relatives how they measured weight when they were young and compare what they did with what you do today.	The student will be able to investigate how specific methods of measuring weight have changed over time.	Specific measurement strategies and tools	Geography 3–5	Recalls various methods and tools used to measure distance (e.g., miles, kilometers, time, cost, perception).

	Task	Objective	Knowledge Focus	Subject, Grade	Benchmark Statement
Mental Procedure: Process	We have been using a variety of types of Internet databases. In fact, the Internet has not been around that long. What were some of the earlier versions of Internet databases? How have they changed?	The student will be able to investigate the early origins of Internet databases.	The use of Internet databases	Technology 6–8	Uses multiple Internet databases in order to expand on issues of interest.
	We have been studying various uses of recurrent relationships to model real-world problems. Using the Internet and other sources, identify the origins of this idea. Who first started using the term *recurrent relationships?* What types of real-world problems were they dealing with?	The student will be able to investigate the origins of the concept of recurrent relations.	The process of modeling and solving real-world problems using recurrent relations	Math 9–12	Uses recurrence relations (i.e., formulas expressing a pattern in which each term is a function of one or more of the previous terms, as in the Fibonacci sequence) to model and to solve real-world problems (e.g., home mortgages, annuities).
Psychomotor Procedure: Skill	Compare the design of the straight and narrow skis of the 1980s with the parabolic skis of today. How and why does the design change impact the way the skis are used to make a turn? Use accounts by expert skiers to answer this question.	The student will be able to investigate how and why changes in sports equipment can impact skill required in the sport.	Specific skiing techniques	Physical Education 9–12	Uses advanced sport-specific skills (e.g., aquatics, dance, individual and team sports).

(Continued)

113

Figure 6.5 (Continued)

	Task	Objective	Knowledge Focus	Subject, Grade	Benchmark Statement
	Describe various techniques people use for keeping on pitch. Which one seems best to you? Use opinions expressed by professional performers to address the issue.	The student will be able to investigate techniques for keeping on pitch.	The skill of keeping on pitch	Music 6–8	Uses breath control, expression, and technical accuracy when singing (e.g., uses appropriate timbre, intonation, diction, pitches, and rhythms) and sings at a level that includes range and changes of tempo, key, and meter.
Psychomotor Procedure: Process	Identify a rule change in the past decade of professional football that has had an impact in the way that certain plays are executed or when they are called. What was the intention of the rule change? Has it been effective?	The student will be able to investigate how changes in a sport's rules can have an impact on play.	The process and rules regarding a specific sport	Physical Education 9–12	Follows appropriate rules for a select sport and applies offensive and defensive strategies.
	Investigate the process for making an oil painting during the Renaissance and how artists make them today. What techniques have remained the same over the centuries, and why do they continue to be in use today?	The student will be able to investigate the characteristics of art media and how they have changed or remained the same over time.	The process of making an oil painting	Visual Arts 5–8	Understands how communication of experiences and ideas can be affected by different uses of art media, techniques, and processes.

Investigating With Psychomotor Procedures

Psychomotor skills and processes can be the subject of investigating tasks. For example, the first investigating task for psychomotor skills asks students to collect information about the impact of parabolic skis on the procedure of making turns. Students are asked to use opinions from expert skiers. The first example of an investigating task involving psychomotor processes addresses rules for playing a specific sport. Students must examine how changes in these rules have affected the sport.

SUMMARY OF KEY POINTS FOR KNOWLEDGE UTILIZATION OBJECTIVES AND TASKS

Decision-Making Objectives and Tasks

- Require students to select among alternatives
- Use terms and phrases like the following: decide, select the best among the following alternatives, which among the following would be best, what is the best way, which of these is most suitable
- Use short and extended written and oral constructed-response formats
- Use specific graphic organizers

Problem-Solving Objectives and Tasks

- Require students to overcome an obstacle to a goal
- Use terms and phrases like the following: solve, how would you overcome, adapt, develop a strategy to, figure out a way to, how will you reach your goal under these conditions
- Use short and extended written and oral constructed-response formats

Experimenting Objectives and Tasks

- Require students to generate and test hypotheses
- Use terms and phrases like the following: generate and test, test the idea that, what would happen if, how would you test it, how would you determine if, how can this be explained, based on this explanation what can be predicted
- Use short and extended written and oral constructed-response formats

Investigating Objectives and Tasks

- Require students to test hypotheses using what others have said or written as data as opposed to observational data they collect themselves

- Use terms and phrases like the following: investigate, research, find out about, take a position on, what are the defining features of, how did this happen, why did this happen, what would have happened if
- Use short and extended written and oral constructed-response formats

CHAPTER SEVEN

Metacognition
Objectives and Tasks

The metacognitive processes oversee learning. There are four categories of metacognitive processes: (1) specifying goals, (2) process monitoring, (3) monitoring clarity, and (4) monitoring accuracy.

SPECIFYING GOALS

The metacognitive process of specifying goals involves setting specific goals relative to one's understanding or skill at a specific type of knowledge and developing a plan for accomplishing the goals. Figure 7.1 lists specifying goals objectives and tasks for the various domains of knowledge.

The phrase *set goals* is frequently used in specifying goals, objectives, and tasks along with terms and phrases like the following:

- What would you like to accomplish
- Identify something you want to

Specifying goals involves setting goals for specific types of knowledge and also identifying how those goals might be accomplished. To demonstrate goal specification, a student must not only articulate a goal relative to a specific knowledge component but also articulate the specifics of a plan for accomplishing the goal.

The most common format for specifying goals tasks is short or extended written and oral constructed response. A graphic organizer like that in Figure 7.2 can be used to aid students in the process of specifying goals.

Although very simple in nature, the graphic organizer in Figure 7.2 requires students to identify a goal, outline a plan for accomplishing the goal,

Figure 7.1 Specifying Goals Objectives and Tasks

	Task	Objective	Knowledge Focus	Subject, Grade	Benchmark Statement
Information: Details: Terms, Facts, Time sequences	What is a goal you have or might have relative to your understanding of the sequence of events leading to the Second World War? What would you have to do reach your goal?	The student will be able to set a goal relative to understanding the sequence of events in World War II and identify how it can be accomplished.	Sequence of events in WWII	U.S. History 7–8	Understands the series of events that led up to World War II (e.g., the legacy of World War I, the depression in the United States, ethnic and ideological conflicts, imperialism, and traditional political or economic rivalries) and the events of the war itself (e.g., the reasons for early Axis power victories between 1939 and 1942, how Hitler used the despair of the German people to rise to power).
	What is a goal you have or might have relative to your understanding of the roles and responsibilities of the different branches of our government? What would you have to do to reach your goal?	The student will be able to set a goal relative to understanding the three branches of government and identify how that goal can be accomplished.	Details regarding the three branches of government	Civics 6–8	Understands the main powers and functions of each branch of government in a system of shared powers (e.g., legislative, executive, judicial) and the working relationships between the branches.
Information: Organizing Generalization	What is a goal you have or might have relative to your understanding of how people act differently in a group from how they act when they are on their own? What would you have to do to reach your goal?	The student will be able to set a goal relative to understanding how members of a group behave and identify how that goal can be accomplished.	Generalizations about how members of a group behave	Behavioral Studies 3–5	Understands that individuals can be influenced to do things they would not otherwise do (good or bad) when they are members of a group.

	Task	Objective	Knowledge Focus	Subject, Grade	Benchmark Statement
	What is a goal you have or might have relative to your understanding of how the principles of energy transfer in and out of the atmosphere help explain variation in weather and climate? What would you have to do reach your goal?	The student will be able to set a goal relative to understanding the transfer of energy in and out of the atmosphere and identify how that goal can be accomplished.	Principles regarding the transfer of energy	Science 9–12	Understands how weather and climate are affected by heat and energy transfer in and out of the atmosphere (e.g., radiation, conduction, convection–advection).
Mental Procedure: Skill	What is a goal you have or might have relative to your ability to use specific functions in a GPS device? How might you reach this goal?	The student will be able to set a goal relative to the ability to use specific functions in a GPS device and identify how that goal can be reached.	Use of specific functions in a GPS device	Geography 9–12	Understands the elements and uses of geographic technologies (e.g., geographic information systems [GIS] and satellite-produced imagery).
	What is a goal you have or might have relative to your ability to perform basic mental computations? How might you reach this goal?	The student will be able to set a goal relative to the ability to perform mental calculations and identify how that goal can be reached.	Performing mental calculations	Math 3–5	Performs basic mental addition and subtraction computations involving whole numbers.
Mental Procedure: Process	What is a goal you have or might have about your ability to better understand what you are reading? How might you reach this goal?	The student will be able to set a goal relative to the ability to comprehend texts and identify how that goal can be reached.	The process of comprehending text	Language Arts K–2	Uses organizational features (e.g., picture captions, title, headings, story structure, story topic) to aid understanding and make predictions about content (e.g., action, events, resolutions).
	What is a goal you have or might have relative to your ability to use a variety of sentences to communicate your thoughts? How might you reach this goal?	The student will be able to set a goal relative to using a variety of sentence types in a composition and identify how that goal can be reached.	The process of using a variety of sentences when writing	Language Arts 6–8	Uses all sentence types fluidly with an eye for elaborating ideas (e.g., simple, compound, and complex sentences; parallel structure, such as similar grammatical forms or juxtaposed items).

(Continued)

Figure 7.1 (Continued)

	Task	Objective	Knowledge Focus	Subject, Grade	Benchmark Statement
Psychomotor Procedure: Skill	What is a goal you have or might have relative to your ability to master a serve or pass in a favorite sport? How might you reach this goal?	The student will be able to set a goal relative to the ability to master a serve or pass in a specific sport and identify how that goal can be reached.	The skill of passing or serving	Physical Education 7–8	Understands movements associated with highly skilled athletes (e.g., what moves make a successful tennis serve).
	What is a goal you have or might have about using a computer keyboard? How might you reach this goal?	The student will be able to set a goal relative to using a computer keyboard and identify how that goal can be reached.	Keyboarding	Technology 6–8	Types with progressing proficiency, showing some key memorization.
	What is a goal you have or might have about using the correct pronunciation in Spanish? How might you reach this goal?	The student will be able to set a goal regarding correct pronunciation in Spanish and identify how that goal can be reached.	The skill of using correct pronunciation	Foreign Language K–4	Uses language mechanics, conventions and style (e.g., grammar, spelling, vocabulary, dialect, slang, idioms, humor, pronunciation, intonation, tone, stress, structure) appropriate for different audiences (e.g., peers, teachers) and settings (e.g., formal, informal).
Psychomotor Procedure: Process	What is a goal you have or might have about performing an instrumental piece while others sing or play contrasting parts? How might you reach this goal?	The student will be able to set a goal regarding an instrumental piece as accompaniment and identify how that goal can be reached.	The process of performing an instrumental piece	Music 3–5	Performs instrumental parts with others in an orchestralike setting (e.g., simple rhythmic or melodic ostinatos, contrasting rhythmic lines, harmonic progressions and chords).
	What is a goal you have or might have about achieving a specific effect in painting? How might you reach this goal?	The student will be able to set a goal relative to achieving a specific effect in painting and identify how that goal can be reached.	The process of achieving a specific effect when painting	Visual Arts 5–8	Understands how communication of experiences and ideas can be affected by different uses of art media, techniques, and processes.

Figure 7.2   Graphic Organizer for Specifying Goals

My goal:

My plan: _____

_____

_____

_____

Resources I will need:

and identify the resources necessary for executing the plan. Across all the domains of knowledge, it is the student's response to the question regarding the manner in which the goal will be accomplished that provides insight into the level at which the student is employing the metacognitive process of specifying goals. For example, a response in which the student notes, "I will have to work harder to accomplish this goal" does not truly address the metacognitive process of goal setting. Rather, the student should identify a clear objective, a rough time line, necessary resources and the like.

Specifying Goals With Information

Specifying goals tasks for details and organizing ideas involve setting goals for specific details and organizing ideas along with a plan for accomplishing those goals. For example, the first specifying goals task for details addresses details about World War II. Students must set a goal relative to increasing their knowledge regarding this information and establish a plan for doing so. The first specifying goals task for organizing ideas deal with setting goals regarding generalizations about how members of a group behave.

Specifying Goals With Mental Procedures

Specifying goals tasks for mental skills and processes involve setting goals for specific mental skills and processes along with a plan for accomplishing those goals. For example, the first specifying goals task for mental skills involves use of specific functions on a GPS device. Students must set a goal relative to these skills and establish a plan for accomplishing the goal. The first specifying goals task for mental processes involves setting goals regarding the process of comprehending text.

Specifying Goals With Psychomotor Procedures

Specifying goals tasks for psychomotor skills and processes involve setting goals for specific psychomotor skills and processes along with a plan for accomplishing those goals. For example, the first specifying goals task for psychomotor skills involves the skill of passing or serving in a specific sport. Students must set a goal for improving their performance in these skills and then establish a plan for accomplishing the goal. The first specifying goals task for psychomotor processes involves setting goals relative to performing an instrumental piece.

PROCESS MONITORING

Process monitoring commonly involves determining how effectively a plan for accomplishing a goal is being accomplished and how effectively a procedure is being carried out in real time, particularly when a goal has been established for the procedure. The goals addressed in process monitoring might be relatively long-term goals established by the metacognitive process of specifying goals or they might be relatively short-term goals established for a specific situation. Figure 7.3 presents process monitoring objectives and tasks across the various domains of knowledge.

The term *monitor* is commonly used in process monitoring tasks along with terms and phrases like the following:

- Evaluate
- Determine how well
- Determine how effectively

(*Text continues on page 129*)

Figure 7.3   Process Monitoring Objectives and Tasks

Task	Objective	Knowledge Focus	Subject, Grade	Benchmark Statement
Information: Details: Terms, Facts, Time sequences				
We have been studying aspects of economics related to intended and unintended consequences. As we've learned, the term *externalities* describes unintended consequences that might be beneficial or harmful to others. Set a goal regarding your understanding of this term. As you undertake this, observe how you refine your understanding. What works best for you? Definitions, examples, or actual cases? If in the process you find yourself confused, what do you think might have gone wrong in your approach?	The student will be able to monitor how well he or she is refining his or her understanding relative to the term *externalities* based on a personal goal he or she has set.	A specific economics term	Economics 9–12	Knows that *externalities* can be defined as unintentional effects (good or bad) that result when production or consumption of a particular good or service affects people who are not directly involved in the market exchange (e.g., a negative externality occurs in production when large companies exploit workers in poor countries to make cheaper products; a positive externality in production occurs when drugs made to treat one medical condition are found to help treat another as well).
There are many types of terrain—marsh, alpine, and tundra, just to name a few. See if you can develop a personal system, a schema, or categories that will help you better understand the differences among these terms and why they provide useful distinctions. As you gain a better understanding, watch what it is you do that seems to be most helpful and what doesn't seem to work. Can you say what works, what doesn't, and why?	Based on a personally set goal, the student will be able to monitor how well his or her understanding about the differences among terms used to describe terrain.	Specific geography terms	Geography 9–12	Understands the advantages and disadvantages of using places for different activities based on their physical characteristics (e.g., flood zone, forest, tundra, earthquake zone, river crossing).

(Continued)

Figure 7.3 (Continued)

	Task	Objective	Knowledge Focus	Subject, Grade	Benchmark Statement
Information: Organizing Generalization	It's a truism that transportation and communication can have a significant impact on how people live and relate to one another. As you develop the examples, identify what helps you understand these ideas better. When you find examples that don't help your understanding, see if you can describe what it is about the examples that don't serve the purpose.	The student will be able to monitor how well he or she is meeting a personal goal regarding learning generalizations about transportation and communication.	Generalizations about transportation and communication	Geography 3–5	Knows how updates in transportation and communication technology have affected relationships between people or communities in different locations.
Information: Organizing Principle	We've been discussing some of the science associated with global warming. We learned of the principle that warm air holds more moisture than cool air. Set a goal about learning more about this idea in terms of its implications for global warming and climate. In other words, what impact does this principle suggest if temperature is rising across the globe? As you seek to learn about this, keep aware about what helps you understand—what ways you find help you make the connections—and also any approaches you use that do not help you understand the problem.	The student will be able to monitor a goal he or she has set regarding understanding the principle that warm air holds more moisture than cool air and its implications for climate.	A principle regarding the amount of moisture air holds at different temperatures	Science 6–8	Understands the elements of the water cycle (e.g., evaporation, condensation, precipitation, runoff, percolation) and their effects on the climate and weather patterns.

124

	Task	Objective	Subject, Grade	Knowledge Focus	Benchmark Statement
Mental Procedure: Skill	The years 1864 and 1865 were some of the most eventful in the Civil War. Construct a time line that organizes these events and set standards regarding the information you time line will contain. How does this process of organizing help you better understand the impact these events had on the people of that time? Consider whether this time line has some disadvantages. For example, might it give the misimpression that each event caused the event that followed?	The student will be able to monitor how well his or her time line for the Civil War has met the standard he or she has established.	U.S. History 7–8	Use of a time line	Knows the events that shaped the Civil War and its outcome (e.g., differences between the economic, technological, and human resources of the Union and Confederate sides; the impact of the Emancipation Proclamation).
	Translating story problems into symbolic forms is an important step to finding a solution. Review the several story problems provided, focusing less on the answer than the way that you think about the story in order to identify the variables and how they are related. Set a goal for your understanding of this process. Is there an approach that seems to work better than another? Check your formulas against the ones provided. What worked and what didn't? Do you know why?	The student will be able to monitor how well he or she has met a personal goal regarding his or her understanding of the skill of representing story problems symbolically.	Math 3–5	Representing story problems symbolically	Translates problem situations into a variety of forms (e.g., a graph to a symbolic expression).

(Continued)

Figure 7.3 (Continued)

	Task	Objective	Knowledge Focus	Subject, Grade	Benchmark Statement
Mental Procedure: Process	You've been provided with a sheet divided in three columns. The left-most column has five rows, each with the same foreign language passage. Starting with the first blank column on the top row, provide a rough translation. Underline those words in the passage of the first column that helped you come to this translation. In the third, far right column, make any notes about what words or phrases are still unclear. For each row, and for as many rows as necessary, refine your translation in the second column, underlining the new parts of the passage that you have addressed, and making notes in the third column about your progress. For example, in the first row, you might make a note about how you used the vocabulary words you know to draft your first translation. By the last row, you might be talking about connecting words or understanding how phrases are linked together. Before you actually begin the process, set a personal goal for yourself and then see how well you met your goal.	The student will be able to monitor his or her progress in meeting a personal goal regarding translating a foreign language passage.	The process of translating a foreign language passage	Foreign Language 5–8	Understands the content of various appropriate sources on familiar topics (e.g., personal letters, brochures, illustrated newspaper and magazine articles, advertisements).

Task	Objective	Knowledge Focus	Subject, Grade	Benchmark Statement
Select one of the books we have in our class library and use all the meaning clues we have been learning—the title, the topic, the pictures and picture captions—to help you understand the story. After you read the story, we will discuss how all these clues helped you understand the story better, or if they didn't, why they didn't.	The student will be able to monitor how well he or she is using meaning clues to understand a story.	The process of using meaning clues to understand a story	Language Arts K–2	Uses textual clues (e.g., captions, title, headings, story structure) to aid comprehension and make predictions about content (e.g., action, events, resolution).
Psychomotor Procedure: Skill				
Improvise a harmonizing part that is stylistically appropriate for a specific song. Set a goal for your performance before you begin. Record your improvisation and listen to it, noting the sections that were successful and those that were less successful. How well did you meet your goal? Can you determine what techniques were most useful? Try the task again to see if your improvisation is better or more appropriate for the music.	The student will be able to monitor how well he or she is learning to improvise harmony that is appropriate for a specific style of music.	Harmonizing within a specific type of music	Music 9–12	Harmonizes in appropriate style.

(Continued)

Figure 7.3 (Continued)

	Task	Objective	Knowledge Focus	Subject, Grade	Benchmark Statement
	On your next ski run, select one aspect of your skiing as a focus, such as your orientation to the fall line, the shape of each carve, or your stance coming into and out of a turn. Set a specific goal for yourself. What do you observe about the skill that you do well, and what might you need to work more on? How did your attention to the task help or distract from your execution of the skill?	The student will be able to monitor how well he or she meets a personal goal for executing a specific skiing skill.	A sport-specific skill	Physical Education 9–12	Uses appropriate skills in selected sports or activities (e.g., swimming, ballet, hiking, tennis, baseball).
Psychomotor Procedure: Process	As you start the next art project, keep a journal that identifies your initial plans for producing the art piece, what techniques or processes you used and why, and whether you had to make changes in your approach to meet your goal. Describe what you learned from this process that might help you next time you begin a project.	The student will be able to monitor how well he or she meets a goal relative to executing the processes necessary to produce an art piece.	The process of producing a piece of art	Visual Arts 5–8	Knows how the expression of experiences and ideas can be shaped using the qualities and characteristics of different art media.
	Choose three different dance elements we have learned and combine them into a smooth sequence that suits the music provided. Before you begin, set a personal goal for what you want to accomplish. Try different sequences to find which seem to work best. Describe why you made your final choices.	The student will be able to monitor how well he or she reaches a personal goal relative to combining dance sequences that are smooth and suit the music provided.	The process of combining dance sequences	Dance 5–8	Understands movement elements observed in dance and understands appropriate dance vocabulary (e.g., level, direction).

Process monitoring tasks are frequently extended in their duration, particularly if the focus is a long-term goal. In such cases, they require students to keep track of learning over time and report on how well they have met their long-term goals. The most common response format for process monitoring tasks is short or extended written or oral constructed response.

Process Monitoring With Information

Process monitoring tasks for information involve monitoring the extent to which goals are being met in terms of understanding specific details and organizing ideas. For example, the first process monitoring task for details in Figure 7.3 addresses a specific economics term. To complete the task, students must monitor their progress in meeting a specific goal they have set for learning that term. The first process monitoring task for organizing ideas addresses generalizations about transportation and communication. Again students set personal goals regarding their understanding and then monitor their progress toward those goals.

Process Monitoring With Mental Procedures

To elicit process monitoring for mental and psychomotor procedures, tasks must be designed in such a way that students can monitor how well they are meeting goals relative to the execution of these procedures. For example, the first process monitoring task for mental skills involves using a time line. Students must articulate standards for their time lines and the extent to which the finished product meets their standards. The first process monitoring task for mental processes involves the process of translating a foreign language passage. Students set explicit goals for translating the passage and then determine how well their goals were met.

Process Monitoring With Psychomotor Procedures

Process monitoring for psychomotor procedures follows the same pattern as process monitoring with mental procedures. The first process monitoring task for psychomotor skills involves harmonizing within a specific type of music. Students must record their attempts at harmonizing so that they might analyze how well they have met their goals. The first process monitoring task for psychomotor processes involves producing a piece of art. Goals are set, and progress towards those goals is monitored.

MONITORING CLARITY

As its name implies, monitoring clarity involves determining the extent to which an individual is clear about specific aspects of knowledge. *Clarity* is defined here as being free from indistinction or ambiguity. Stated in more positive terms, one who is clear about knowledge can recognize the distinctions important to that knowledge and ascribe precise meaning to each important distinction.

Figure 7.4 presents monitoring clarity objectives and tasks across the various domains of knowledge.

Commonly terms and phrases like the following are employed in monitoring clarity objectives and tasks:

- What are you clear about
- What are you unclear about
- How could you better understand

The most common format for monitoring clarity tasks is short or extended written and oral constructed-response formats.

Across all domains of knowledge, the more precise students can be about their areas of lack of clarity, the more they are exercising the metacognitive process of monitoring clarity. For example, one level of monitoring for clarity regarding the mental process of using WordPerfect® would be demonstrated by the following student response:

"I get confused when I try to center things."

However, a much deeper level of metacognitive awareness would be exhibited by the following response:

"I don't understand how you can go back and center a line in the middle of a document without losing all the margins that you have already set up."

Below we consider monitoring clarity tasks across the domains of knowledge.

Monitoring Clarity With Information

Monitoring clarity tasks for the domain of information involve identifying how clear a student is about specific details and organizing ideas. For example, the first monitoring clarity task for details involves details about the human skeletal structure. Students must determine their level of clarity about the specific role it plays in growth and survival. The first monitoring clarity task for organizing ideas addresses clarity regarding generalizations about specific substances.

(*Text continues on page 135*)

Figure 7.4 Monitoring Clarity Objectives and Tasks

	Task	Objective	Knowledge Focus	Subject, Grade	Benchmark Statement
Information: Details: Terms, Facts, Time sequences	Think about the skeletal structure of the human body. Are you clear about the specific role it plays in growth and survival? What is not clear to you?	The student will be able to identify details about the skeletal structure about which he or she has difficulty making distinctions.	Details about the human skeletal structure	Science 3–5	Understands that the growth, survival, and reproduction of living organisms depend upon distinct body structures and body systems (e.g., one body structure is conducive to swimming while another is conducive to flying).
	We have studied the Age of Discovery and noted that that period is significant for the exchange of flora, fauna, and pathogens. What aspects about this exchange are unclear to you?	The student will be able to identify details about the Age of Discovery about which he or she has difficulty making distinctions.	Details about the Age of Discovery	World History 7–8	Knows the effects of the interactions of flora, fauna, and pathogens on both local and global populations (e.g., how the disease microorganisms the Pilgrims brought devastated indigenous populations; population trends and growth in the Americas, Europe, and East Asia in the sixteenth and seventeenth centuries; origins and routes of flora and fauna exchanged across the world).
Information: Organizing Generalization	Do you know which substances are helpful and which are harmful? Some substances, like prescription drugs, can be helpful for some people but harmful for others. Which substances are you confused about?	The student will be able to identify those aspects of harmful and helpful substances about which he or she is unclear.	Generalizations about specific substances	Health K–2	Understands how to tell the difference between helpful and harmful substances.

(Continued)

131

Figure 7.4 (Continued)

	Task	Objective	Knowledge Focus	Subject, Grade	Benchmark Statement
Information: Organizing Principle	Tensions between individual freedoms and rights and national security are not academic. In the course of U.S. history to the present day, there are differing views as to when or even whether it is acceptable to give up certain rights for security. Are you clear about where the line is for you? Explain.	The student will be able to identify those aspects of the tension between individual freedom and national security about which he or she is uncertain.	Principles regarding the relationship between individual freedoms and security	Civics 9–12	Knows how U.S. constitutional values and principles affect U.S. foreign policy (e.g., a commitment to the self-determination of nations) and understands the strains that are created among U.S. values and interests as we face the necessity of international politics (e.g., a commitment to human rights and the requirements of national security).
Mental Procedure: Skill	Consider the different ways that data can be represented. How can changes of scale for different representations affect the immediate message communicated? Is it clear how the same data can be interpreted differently because of the manner of presentation? Explain.	The student will be able to identify areas of uncertainty about how the use of scale can affect data presentation.	Specific skills involved in selecting and using a scale to present data	Math 6–8	Understands that tables, graphs, and symbols can all be used to represent the same set of data and that these different methods often convey different messages (e.g., variation in scale can alter a visual message).
	We have been studying how to think about the beginning and ending of words—prefixes and suffixes—to help figure out what the words mean. Are you clear why this is useful and why sometimes it is not useful? Go through the provided word list and see if you are clear about when it works, when it doesn't, and why.	The student will be able to identify when he or she is unclear whether a prefix or suffix can be helpful in decoding a word meaning.	A specific decoding skill	Language Arts K–2	Decodes words by using basic structural analysis (e.g., syllables, prefixes, suffixes, basic roots and root words, spelling patterns).

	Task	Objective	Knowledge Focus	Subject, Grade	Benchmark Statement
Mental Procedure: Process	How is the cartogram different from other thematic maps? Why would you choose it over other types of map to represent data? What characteristics of a cartogram do you need to become clearer about?	The student will be able to identify any uncertainty he or she has regarding the best use of a cartogram to represent data.	The various processes for modeling thematic maps	Geography 6–8	Uses thematic maps (e.g., patterns of population and disease, vegetation, economic features) and understands the elements and uses of cartograms.
	We use permutation and combination to solve counting problems. Are you clear about which should be used when? What don't you understand about how they can be used to solve problems?	The student will be able to identify any uncertainty he or she has regarding the use of permutations as opposed to combinations to solve counting problems.	The process of using permutations and combinations to solve counting problems	Math 9–12	Understands counting procedures and reasoning (e.g., how to find the number of ways to arrange objects in a set, use of permutations and combinations to solve counting problems).
Psychomotor Procedure: Skill	For a sport that you enjoy that requires striking a ball, consider what you know about the ideal hand and foot position and follow-through. What aspects are you not clear about? Are there advantages to approaches you might not be using?	The student will be able to identify those aspects of the proper form for striking a ball about which he or she is unclear.	The skill of striking a ball within a specific sport	Physical Education 7–8	Understands movement associated with highly skilled athletes (e.g., moves that make a successful hit in baseball).
	We need to make sure that we use smooth transitions from running and jumping. Think through what it takes to ensure that the process is smooth. Is there something you're not clear about?	The student will be able to identify those aspects of transitions between sequential motor skills about which he or she is uncertain.	The skill of transitioning between specific motor skills	Physical Education K–2	Transitions between motor skills used in a sequence (e.g., going from running into a slide).

(Continued)

Figure 7.4 (Continued)

	Task	Objective	Knowledge Focus	Subject, Grade	Benchmark Statement
Psychomotor Procedure: Process	For a specific net or invasion game that you play, consider the strategies you use, for example, for preventing an opponent from stealing the ball in basketball or placing the ball away from an opponent in a racket sport. Consider whether these strategies are always good, regardless of the type of opponent. How can you be clearer about when these strategies are best used?	The student will be able to identify areas of uncertainty about strategy use during invasion games.	The process of playing invasion games	Physical Education 3–6	Uses beginning strategies for net and invasion games (e.g., keeping the ball going, keeping the ball away from an opponent, preventing an opponent from stealing the ball).
	Consider the challenge of interacting as an invented character in an improvised script. Are you clear about what would change in the improvisation and what characteristics you should maintain to keep the character unified? Explain.	The student will be able to identify those aspects of improvisation about which he or she is uncertain.	The physical aspects of the process of improvisation	Theatre 5–8	Plays a character in both improvised and scripted situations.

Monitoring Clarity With Mental Procedures

Monitoring clarity tasks for the domain of mental procedures involve identifying how clear a student is about specific mental skills and processes. For example, the first monitoring clarity task for mental skills requires students to identify their level of certainty regarding how the use of scale can affect data presentation. The first monitoring clarity task for mental processes involves clarity regarding various processes for reading thematic maps.

Monitoring Clarity With Psychomotor Procedures

Monitoring clarity tasks for the domain of psychomotor procedures involve identifying how clear a student is about specific psychomotor skills and processes. For example, the first monitoring clarity task for psychomotor skills requires students to identify their level of clarity regarding the skill of striking a ball within a specific sport. The first monitoring clarity task for psychomotor processes involves clarity relative to the process of playing invasion games.

MONITORING ACCURACY

Monitoring accuracy involves determining the extent to which an individual is correct in terms of his understanding of specific knowledge. Monitoring accuracy is distinct from, but related to, monitoring clarity. That is, a student could be clear about some aspects of knowledge—have no ambiguity or lack of distinction—but in fact be inaccurate. It is important to contrast the metacognitive process of monitoring accuracy with the analysis process of analyzing errors since they both address inaccuracies and errors. Analyzing errors involves the errors made by others as well as oneself. Monitoring accuracy deals exclusively with one's own inaccuracies or errors. In addition, monitoring accuracy involves checking one's assumptions regarding accuracy. For example, a student might believe he or she is accurate in his or her understanding of the position of a political candidate. However, when executing the metacognitive process of monitoring accuracy, he or she would actually check to determine if the assumptions about the candidate's position are in fact accurate. Error analysis does not involve this "checking one's assumptions" aspect.

Figure 7.5 lists tasks for monitoring accuracy across the three knowledge domains of knowledge.

As Figure 7.5 illustrates, a critical aspect of monitoring accuracy is defending or verifying one's judgment of accuracy. This implies that students must not only make judgments about their accuracy but also must provide evidence for this judgment.

(*Text continues on page 140*)

Figure 7.5 Monitoring Accuracy Objectives and Tasks

	Task	Objective	Knowledge Focus	Subject, Grade	Benchmark Statement
Information: Details: Terms, Facts, Time sequences	We have discussed the distinction between the terms *true correlation* and *believable correlation*. What aspects about this distinction do you believe? Check to make sure you understand accurately.	The student will be able to identify and defend the extent to which he or she is accurate about the terms *true correlation* and *believable correlation*.	Specific mathematics terminology	Math 9–12	Understands the basic concept of correlation (e.g., a true correlation versus a believable correlation; how to know when two variables are correlated).
	We've learned that foreign vocabulary words can be easy to learn when they are related to English words, as Spanish *fruta* is to English *fruit*. But false cognates, sometimes called false friends, make it difficult to remember the true meaning of a word. For example, Spanish *assistir* means *to attend*. The English word *assist* is *ayudar* in Spanish. Attached is a list of terms that include both true and false cognates. Which can you identify correctly? How do you know you are correct?	The student will be able to identify and explain why he or she believes a specific word to be a true or a false cognate.	Specific foreign language terminology	Foreign Language K–4	Knows common cognates and expressions in both the language being studied and any native languages.
Information: Organizing Generalization	Select a recent decision that you have made or you have watched someone else make. Identify whether you are accurate in your identification of the opportunity cost for this decision. How do you know you are accurate? Check your understanding.	The student will be able to identify and defend his or her accuracy in providing an example of an opportunity cost.	Generalizations about opportunity cost	Economics 6–8	Understands the necessity of opportunity costs and that effective economic decision making includes comparing the costs and benefits associated with other possible choices.

	Task	Objective	Knowledge Focus	Subject, Grade	Benchmark Statement
Information: Organizing Principle	Are you accurate about identifying examples in daily life of conduction, convection, and radiation? How are you sure that these are valid examples? Check your reasoning.	The student will be able to identify and defend his or her accuracy in selecting daily-life illustrations of conduction, convection and radiation.	Principles regarding conduction, convection, and radiation	Science 6–8	Knows that convection, conduction, and radiation are all ways that heat energy flows from warmer materials or regions to cooler ones.
Mental Procedure: Skill	The problem presented to you required the use of a specific method of indirect measurement. What parts of the process do you know you managed correctly? How do you know you were correct? Check the steps that you have used.	The student will be able to identify and defend the extent to which he or she understands specific techniques for indirect measurement.	Specific techniques regarding indirect measurement	Math 9–12	Selects and uses an appropriate method of measurement (direct or indirect) for a particular situation (e.g., uses properties of similar triangles to measure indirectly the height of an object).
	For three of the multiple choice items, you had to estimate the answer. Were you correct in the selection and use of your estimation strategy? How do you know? Check your strategy.	The student will be able to identify and explain why the estimation strategy he or she selected was used correctly.	Specific estimation strategies	Math 3–5	Estimates computations using specific strategies (e.g., front-end estimation, rounding) and checks accuracy.
Mental Procedure: Process	To what extent are you correct in your use of the GPS across the many different situations we have been studying? How do you know you have used it correctly?	The student will be able to identify and defend the extent to which he or she correctly used a GPS device in a variety of situations.	The general process of using a GPS device	Geography 9–12	Understands the elements and uses of geographic technologies (e.g., geographic information systems (GIS) and satellite-produced imagery).

(Continued)

Figure 7.5 (Continued)

	Task	Objective	Knowledge Focus	Subject, Grade	Benchmark Statement
	When you reviewed the advertisements that were presented, to what extent were you accurate in your identification of exaggerated claims, glittering generalities, or other attempts to persuade you? How do you know you were accurate? Provide evidence for your conclusions.	The student will be able to identify and defend the extent to which he or she can spot strategies used in advertisements to persuade the consumer.	The process of persuasion in advertising	Language Arts 6–8	Knows methods used in visual media to convince or appeal to a particular audience (e.g., production techniques, such as designing a news program with an eye for entertainment; persuasive techniques, such as use of biased information or exaggerated claims, portrayal of appealing lifestyles and spectacular generalities).
Psychomotor Procedure: Skill	As you made your presentation in Spanish, did you pronounce each word correctly? How do you know the word was pronounced correctly? Reexamine how you pronounce words.	The student will be able to identify and explain why the Spanish words he or she used in a presentation were pronounced correctly.	The skill of pronouncing a specific word	Foreign Language K–4	Uses language mechanics, conventions and style (e.g., grammar, spelling, sentence structure, vocabulary, dialect, slang or idioms; pronunciation, intonation, tone, stress) appropriate for a variety of audiences (e.g., peers, teachers) and settings (e.g., formal, informal).
	As you form letters of the alphabet, which do you form correctly? Which letters need more work?	The student will be able to identify which letters of the alphabet he or she forms correctly.	The skill of writing specific letters of the alphabet	Language Arts PreK	Writes or copies familiar words (e.g., own name, pet's name).

	Task	Objective	Knowledge Focus	Subject, Grade	Benchmark Statement
Psychomotor Procedure: Process	When you make your class presentation, how well are you using the right tone of voice and volume? Do you follow the rules of effective discussion we have been studying? How do you know?	The student will be able to identify whether he or she modulates tone of voice and volume when making a presentation.	The process of modulating tone and voice when making a presentation	Language Arts K–2	Uses appropriate volume, phrasing, and intonation for various situations requiring oral communication (e.g., small group settings, informal discussions, class discussions, or presentations).
	Have someone record a video as you perform a sport that awards score points (such as gymnastics, horse jumping, or diving). Review your videotaped performance against what you believed you were accomplishing during the performance. Were you accurate in your judgments? Why or why not? Provide evidence for your conclusion.	The student will be able to identify and defend judgments made upon viewing a recorded performance against the judgments he or she made during the performance.	The process of performing a specific sport	Physical Education 9–12	Uses advanced skills tailored to selected sports or activities (e.g., swimming, dance, hiking, tennis, baseball).

Terms and phrases commonly used in monitoring accuracy objectives and tasks include the following:

- About what do you believe you are accurate?
- About what do you believe you might be inaccurate?

The most common format for monitoring accuracy is short or extended written and oral constructed-response tasks.

It is worth noting again that across all domains of knowledge, a critical aspect of monitoring accuracy tasks is that students must verify whether the information they believed to be accurate is in fact accurate. Consequently, monitoring accuracy tasks involve reviewing and checking information previously presented. As we've mentioned before, this is not the case with the analysis process of analyzing errors.

Monitoring Accuracy With Information

Monitoring accuracy tasks in the domain of information require students to determine how accurate they are about specific details and organizing ideas. For example, the first monitoring accuracy task for details involves specific terminology. To complete this task, students must review what has been presented about these terms and compare that information with their current understanding of the terms. The first monitoring accuracy task for organizing ideas involves the perceived accuracy of generalizations about opportunity cost.

Monitoring Accuracy With Mental Procedures

Monitoring accuracy tasks in the domain of mental procedures require students to determine how accurately they execute specific mental skills and processes. For example, the first monitoring accuracy task for mental skills involves a specific skill regarding indirect measurement. Students must determine how accurately they execute the component parts of this skill. The first monitoring accuracy task for mental procedures involves the accuracy of the general process for using a GPS device.

It is important to distinguish monitoring accuracy for procedures with process monitoring for procedures. As described previously in this chapter, the metacognitive skill of process monitoring involves a specific goal. Students must set specific goals regarding a procedure, and then monitor the extent to which these goals are being met. The metacognitive process of monitoring accuracy does not necessarily involve a goal on the part of the students. Rather it simply involves students judging how accurately the steps in a procedure are being executed and checking the validity of their understanding regarding those steps.

Monitoring Accuracy With Psychomotor Procedures

Monitoring accuracy in the domain of psychomotor procedures follows the same pattern as monitoring accuracy with mental procedures. It requires students to judge how accurately they execute specific psychomotor skills and processes and check the accuracy of their judgments. For example, the first monitoring accuracy task for psychomotor skills involves the skill of pronouncing specific words. Students must judge if they are executing this procedure accurately and examine the validity of their judgments. Again this differs from the metacognitive skill of process monitoring because a personal goal is not involved. It differs from analyzing errors because it goes beyond simply examining the results of a procedure. The first monitoring accuracy task for psychomotor processes involves the process of modulating tone and voice while making a presentation.

Summary of Key Points for Metacognitive Objectives and Tasks

Specifying Goals Objectives and Tasks

- Require students to set goals and establish a plan for accomplishing those goals
- Use terms and phrases like the following: set goals, what would you like to accomplish, identify something you want to
- Use short and extended written and oral constructed-response formats

Process Monitoring Objectives and Tasks

- Require students to determine how effectively goals are being met relative to the knowledge domains; goals may be set via the metacognitive process of specifying goals or for a specific situation
- Use terms and phrases like the following: monitor, evaluate, determine how well, determine how effectively
- Use short and extended written and oral constructed-response formats

Monitoring Clarity Objectives and Tasks

- Require students to determine the extent to which they are free from ambiguity and indistinction about specific aspects of knowledge
- Use terms and phrases like the following: what are you sure about, what are you unsure about, how could you better understand
- Use short and extended written and oral constructed-response formats

Monitoring Accuracy Objectives and Tasks

- Require students to determine the extent to which they are accurate about their understanding of knowledge; involves reexamining assumptions about what is correct or accurate
- Use terms and phrases such as the following: about what do you believe you are accurate, about what do you believe you are inaccurate
- Use short and extended written and oral constructed-response tasks

CHAPTER EIGHT

Self-System Objectives and Tasks

Self-system thinking involves determining and analyzing one's motivation to learn new content. As described in Chapter 2, self-system thinking involves four aspects: (1) examining importance, (2) examining efficacy, (3) examining emotional response, and (4) examining motivation.

Examining Importance

The self-system process of examining importance involves analyzing the extent to which one believes that learning specific knowledge is important and then examining one's beliefs relative to that issue. If an individual does not perceive a specific piece of knowledge as important at a personal level, he or she will probably not be highly motivated to learn it.

Figure 8.1 lists objectives and tasks for the self-system process of examining importance across the three knowledge domains.

Examining importance goes beyond simply identifying how important learning specific knowledge is perceived to be. It also involves examining and defending the logic underlying one's thinking. Obviously this latter part of the process is more applicable to older students. Students at the lower grade levels might be expected to articulate how important they perceive something to be and provide some reason for this perception, but they might not be expected to analyze their thinking.

Examining importance objectives or any other type of self-system process are almost never explicit in standards or benchmark statements. As discussed in the next chapter, a district or school would have to elect to make self-system goals an overt part of the curriculum. They will probably not find a mandate to do so in their state and national standards documents.

(Text continues on page 148)

Figure 8.1 Examining Importance Objectives and Tasks

	Task	Objective	Knowledge Focus	Subject, Grade	Benchmark Statement
Information: Details: Terms, Facts, Time sequences	How important do you think it is that you know how other children's lives in the culture we are studying differ from your own? Each of your groups has studied a specific family in a specific country and communicated with them. Why do you think it might be important to understand how different their houses, food and toys are? Does your thinking make sense?	The student will be able to identify the personal importance he or she places on learning how other children's lives are different from his or her own and analyzes the reasoning behind that judgment.	Facts about how specific families live	Foreign Language K–4	Understands utilitarian forms of the studied culture (e.g., toys, clothes, homes, typical diet, currency) and compares them to those in one's native culture.
	How important do you think it is that you understand the kinds of conflicts that arise between values and principles—for example, the specific conflicts between the majority rule and the minority rights we have been studying? Why do you think it might be important to understand these conflicts? Does your thinking make sense?	The student will be able to identify the personal importance he or she places on understanding specific conflicts that arise between values and principles and analyzes the reasoning behind that judgment.	Facts about specific conflicts	Civics 6–8	Understands past conflicts between fundamental values and principles (e.g., conflicts between one person's rights and the common good, conflicts between majority rule and minority rights).
Information: Organizing Generalization	How important do you think it is that you understand that science cannot answer all questions and that technology cannot solve all human problems or meet all human needs? Why do you think it is important to understand this? Do you think your reasons are valid?	The student will be able to identify the personal importance he or she places on understanding that science and technology cannot solve all problems or meet all human needs and analyzes the reasoning behind that judgment.	Generalizations about the limitations of science and technology	Technology 6–8	Understands that science and technology have limitations.

144

	Task	Objective	Knowledge Focus	Subject, Grade	Benchmark Statement
Information: Organizing Principle	How important do you think it is that you understand the properties and relationships among geometric figures? Why do you think it is important to understand them? Does your thinking represent a strong argument?	The student will be able to identify the personal importance he or she places on understanding the properties and relationships among figures and analyzes the reasoning behind that judgment.	Principles about the relationship among geometric figures	Math 9–12	Solves mathematical and real-world problems by using properties of figures and the relationships between them (e.g., uses understanding of arc, chord, tangents, and properties of circles to determine the radius).
Mental Procedure: Skill	We have been studying a specific set of steps for applying a specific event in history to our own lives. Explain why you believe this to be an important skill or why you do not. How valid is your thinking?	The student will be able to determine how important he or she thinks it is to be able to relate events from history to his or her own life.	The skill of relating a specific historical event to one's own life	Historical Understanding 9–12	Understands how to refrain from believing that specific lessons learned in the past will always apply to problems in the present.
	How important is it that you realize when you are in an emergency situation and what you should do about it? Why do you think it is important or not important? Can you provide an example to show why you are correct?	The student will be able to identify the personal importance he or she places on being able to identify an emergency situation.	The skill of recognizing an emergency situation	Health K–2	Understands how to recognize emergency situations and how to respond (e.g., uses a telephone to obtain assistance; identifies and obtains assistance from police officers, fire fighters and trusted adults; treats common injuries, such as scratches, bruises and sunburns).

(Continued)

Figure 8.1 (Continued)

	Task	Objective	Knowledge Focus	Subject, Grade	Benchmark Statement
Mental Procedure: Process	How important is it that you are able to plan and conduct a simple investigation, including systematic observations and reaching a logical conclusion? Why do you think it is or is not important? Can you provide reasons for your conclusions?	The student will be able to identify the personal importance he or she places on planning and conducting an investigation and analyze the reasoning behind that judgment.	The process of planning and conducting a simple investigation	Science 3–5	Designs and carries out simple investigations (e.g., formulates a specific scientific question, makes appropriate observations, develops logical conclusions).
	How important is it that you are able to summarize and paraphrase informational texts, such as conveying the main ideas and critical details? Why do you think you are correct? Explain your thinking.	The student will be able to identify the personal importance he or she places on summarizing and paraphrasing informational texts and analyze the reasoning behind that judgment.	The process of summarizing and paraphrasing informational text	Language Arts 6–8	Uses summary and paraphrasing to enhance understanding of information in text (e.g., arranges information in a logical order; conveys main ideas, essential details, and underlying meaning; uses own words or quoted materials; preserves author's perspective).
Psychomotor Procedure: Skill	We have been practicing scales on our reed instruments. Do you think this is important to do? Why or why not?	The student will be able to explain why he or she thinks playing a scale on a reed instrument is important or why it is not.	Playing a simple scale on a reed instrument	Music K–2	Plays scales on a basic instrument.
	How important is it that you can use art materials safely and responsibly? Why do you think it is important or not important? Can you provide some good reasons?	The student will be able to identify the personal importance he or she places on using art materials safely and analyze the reasoning behind that judgment.	Using art materials safely	Visual Arts K–4	Uses art materials and tools safely and appropriately.

	Task	Objective	Knowledge Focus	Subject, Grade	Benchmark Statement
Psychomotor Procedure: Process	How important do you think it is that you follow the rules and procedures for the physical-activity settings we have been studying? Do you think this is necessary or unnecessary? Explain your reasoning. How well have you thought this through?	The student will be able to identify the personal importance he or she places on following the rules and procedures for physical-activity settings and analyze the reasoning behind that judgment.	Following the rules and procedures for physical activity settings	Physical Education 7–8	Knows why the rules and procedures in settings of physical activity are important.
	How important is it to use different voice levels depending on what setting you are in, like a small-group discussion or a report to the class? Can you provide good reasons for your answer?	The student will be able to identify the personal importance he or she places on using appropriate voice levels depending on the setting and analyze the reasoning behind that judgment.	The process of using a variety of voice levels across different settings	Language Arts K–2	Adjusts volume, phrasing, and intonation according to the situation at hand (e.g., small group settings, informal discussions or class discussions, class presentations).

Terms and phrases like the following are commonly used in examining importance objectives and tasks:

- How important is it to you
- Why do you think it might be important
- Can you provide some reasons why it is important
- How logical is your thinking

The common format for examining importance tasks is short or extended written and oral constructed-response formats.

Examining Importance With Information

Examining importance tasks for the domain of information involve determining how important it is to learn details and organizing ideas and analyzing the logic of those perceptions. For example, the first examining importance task for details involves facts about specific families. Students first identify how important they believe this information to be. Then they consider the logic of their thinking. The first examining importance task for organizing ideas involves perceptions of importance relative to generalizations about science and technology.

Examining Importance With Mental Procedures

Examining importance tasks for the domain of mental procedures involve determining how important it is to learn specific mental skills and processes and analyzing the logic of those perceptions. For example, the first examining importance task for mental skills involves the skill of relating a specific historic event to one's own life. In this case, the teacher has provided students with a series of simple steps or rules to follow. Students must first determine if they perceive this to be an important skill and then analyze their thinking. The first examining importance task for mental processes involves perceptions of importance relative to the process of planning and conducting simple investigations.

Examining Importance With Psychomotor Procedures

Examining importance tasks for the domain of psychomotor procedures involve determining how important it is to learn psychomotor skills and processes and analyzing the logic of these perceptions. For example, the first examining importance task for psychomotor skills involves playing a simple scale on an instrument. Students must identify how important they believe it is to learn how to play scales on a real instrument and then defend their logic. The first examining importance task for psychomotor processes involves perceptions of importance regarding the process of using art materials safely.

EXAMINING EFFICACY

The self-system process of examining efficacy involves examining the extent to which individuals believe they can improve their understanding or competence relative to a specific type of knowledge. It also involves examining their thinking on the issue. If individuals do not believe they can change their competence relative to a specific piece of knowledge, they will probably not be motivated to learn it, even if they perceive it as important. Figure 8.2 lists objectives and tasks for examining efficacy across the three knowledge domains.

Terms and phrases like the following are commonly used in examining efficacy objectives and tasks:

- Can you improve
- How well do you think you can do
- How well can you learn
- How good are you at
- How logical is your thinking

The most common format for examining efficacy tasks is short or extended written and oral constructed-response formats.

Examining Efficacy With Information

Examining efficacy tasks for the domain of information involve identifying beliefs about one's ability to learn details and organizing ideas and then examining the logic of these beliefs. For example, the first examining efficacy task for details involves details about specific international conflicts. Students must determine how capable they believe themselves to be to improve their understanding of these details. They must also explain and defend their thinking. The first examining efficacy task for organizing ideas involves perceptions of efficacy regarding generalizations about how geography has influenced history.

Examining Efficacy With Mental Procedures

Examining efficacy tasks for the domain of mental procedures involve identifying beliefs about one's ability to improve competence at mental skills and processes and analyzing the reasoning behind these perceptions. For example, the first examining efficacy task for mental skills involves the skill of interpreting specific nonverbal skills. Students must determine if they believe they can get better at this skill and the reasons that they believe so. The first examining efficacy task for mental processes involves perceptions of efficacy regarding the process of translating data into maps, graphs, and charts.

(*Text continues on page 154*)

Figure 8.2   Examining Efficacy Objectives and Tasks

	Task	Objective	Knowledge Focus	Subject, Grade	Benchmark Statement
Information: Details: Terms, Facts, Time sequences	We have been studying the Iraq war. Do you think you can improve your understanding of that war? Why or why not? Explain your thinking. How well supported are your conclusions about this?	The student will be able to identify the extent to which he or she believes his or her understanding of the Iraq war can be improved and analyze his or her thinking.	Details about a specific international conflict	Social Studies 9–12	Knows specific details regarding specific international conflicts.
	We have been studying the development of the Supreme Court. Can you deepen your understanding of the significant events that helped shape the Supreme Court in first few decades of the new nation? What reasons do you have for believing this? How valid is your thinking?	The student will be able to identify the extent to which he or she believes his or her understanding of the development of the Supreme Court can be improved and analyze the reasoning behind these beliefs.	Details regarding the development of the U.S. Supreme Court	History 9–12	Knows how the U.S. Supreme Court was established and the significant events that led to its creation (e.g., Chief Justice Marshall, Article III of the Constitution, Judiciary Act of 1789, *Marbury v. Madison*).
Information: Organizing Generalization	We have seen examples of how physical geography has influenced major historic events. Do you believe you can come to a better understanding of this generalization? What reasons do you have for thinking you can or cannot improve your understanding? How good are these reasons?	The student will be able to identify the extent to which he or she believes his or her understanding of how geography has influenced history can be improved and analyze the reasoning behind these beliefs.	Generalizations about how geography has influenced history	Geography 6–8	Understands how major historic events and movements have been affected by both human and geographic factors (e.g., the courses and outcomes of physical conflict, the establishment of the slave trade in North and South Americas, the profitability of the triangle trade due to the locations of wind and ocean currents, the effects of various land survey systems used in the United States).

	Task	Objective	Knowledge Focus	Subject, Grade	Benchmark Statement
Information: Organizing Principle	The motions of the earth and moon explain many phenomena on earth. Can you reach a better understanding of the principles that account for eclipses and tides? Why do you or don't you believe you can have a better understanding than you do now? Explain and defend your thinking.	The student will be able to identify the extent to which he or she believes his or her understanding of how phenomena on earth can be explained by the motions of the earth and moon and analyze the reasoning behind these beliefs.	Principles regarding the motions of the earth	Science 6–8	Understands how phenomena on earth are affected by the cycles and motions of the sun and the moon (e.g., day and night, the seasons of the year, the moon's phases, eclipses, tides).
Mental Procedure: Skill	We have been discussing how to interpret two common nonverbal cues used in conversation. Can you improve your ability to interpret these specific nonverbal cues? Why do you think you can or can't? How well have you thought through this issue?	The student will be able to identify the extent to which he or she believes his or her competence in interpreting specific nonverbal clues can be improved and analyze the reasoning for that belief.	The skill of interpreting specific nonverbal cues	Language Arts 3–5	Understands nonverbal cues used during the course of a conversation.
	This year we have been learning how to add and subtract fractions with unlike denominators. Can you improve your ability in this skill? Why do you think you can or cannot? Explain your thinking.	The student will be able to identify the extent to which he or she believes his or her competence in adding and subtracting fractions with unlike denominators can be improved and analyze the reasoning for that belief.	Adding and subtracting fractions	Math 6–8	Adds and subtracts fractions with like and unlike denominators.
Mental Procedure: Process	We have been working with various ways to translate primary data into maps, graphs, and charts. How well have you mastered this process of translation? Do you think you can improve your approach? Explain the reasoning behind your answer. Does your thinking make sense?	The student will be able to identify the extent to which he or she believes his or her competence in translating data into maps, graphs, and charts can be improved and analyze the reasoning behind that belief.	Translating data into maps, graphs, and charts	Geography 9–12	Translates data into useful maps, charts, and graphs (e.g., charts developed from census data focusing on specific informational topics, cartograms depicting the relative sizes of European countries based on their urban populations).

(Continued)

Figure 8.2 (Continued)

	Task	Objective	Knowledge Focus	Subject, Grade	Benchmark Statement
	We have logged the results of a recent physical-fitness assessment and learned how to interpret them in order to develop individual fitness goals. How well do you understand the information and how well can you develop a fitness goal based on what you understand—can you be more effective? Why do you believe you can or can't improve? Explain your thinking. How good is your thinking on this issue?	The student will be able to identify the extent to which he or she believes his or her competence in using fitness assessment information to develop personal fitness goals can be improved and analyze the reasoning for that belief.	Using fitness assessment information	Physical Education 7–8	Understands how to create fitness goals and plans based on information interpreted from a fitness assessment.
Psychomotor Procedure: Skill	We have been practicing proper fingering for the computer keyboard. Do you think you can get better at this? Why or why not?	The student will be able to identify the extent to which he or she believes his or her competence in fingering for the computer keyboard can be improved and analyze the reasoning for that belief.	Specific keyboarding skills	Technology 3–5	Uses proper fingering (from the home row) and proper posture while using the computer keyboard.
	We have been practicing specific climbing techniques. Select one technique you are having difficulty with. Can you get better at this? Why or why not?	The student will be able to identify the extent to which he or she believes his or her competence in a specific climbing technique can be improved and explain his or her thinking.	A specific climbing technique	Physical Education K–2	Develops muscular strength and endurance by participating in specific activities (e.g., weight lifting, climbing).

	Task	Objective	Knowledge Focus	Subject, Grade	Benchmark Statement
Psychomotor Procedure: Process	We've learned that even nonverbal signs can communicate a great deal to the audience. Can you improve your eye contact, gestures, and posture when you present? Why or why not? Why do you think your beliefs about yourself are accurate?	The student will be able to identify the extent to which he or she believes his or her competence in using nonverbal techniques can be improved and analyze the reasoning for that belief.	The process of using nonverbal communication techniques	Language Arts 3–5	Skillfully communicates nonverbally (e.g., eye contact, hand gestures, facial expressions).
	Identify offensive or defensive strategies in a sport you engage in often. How well do you execute these strategies? Can you get better? Explain why or why not and defend your reasoning.	The student will be able to identify the extent to which he or she believes his or her competence in offensive or defensive strategies can be improved and analyze the reasoning for that belief.	Offensive or defensive strategies in a specific sport	Physical Education 7–8	Uses basic offensive and defensive strategies in an individual or team sport.

Examining Efficacy With Psychomotor Procedures

Examining efficacy tasks for the domain of psychomotor procedures involve identifying beliefs about one's ability to improve competence at psychomotor skills and processes and analyzing the reasoning behind these perceptions. For example, the first examining efficacy task for psychomotor skills involves specific keyboarding skills. Students must determine if they believe they can improve their competence at these psychomotor skills and explain and defend their thinking behind their beliefs. The first examining efficacy task for psychomotor processes involves perceptions of efficacy regarding the process of using nonverbal communication techniques.

EXAMINING EMOTIONAL RESPONSE

The process of examining emotional response involves identifying what emotions, if any, are associated with specific knowledge, whether these emotions interfere with learning, and the logic behind those associations. As described in Chapter 2, negative affect can dampen a student's motivation to learn or improve at something, even if the student believes that the knowledge is important and that he or she has the requisite ability and resources. Figure 8.3 lists objectives and tasks for examining emotional response across the three knowledge domains.

The key feature of this type of self-system thinking is the identification of the logic underlying emotional responses. There is no necessary attempt to change these associations—only to understand them. This said, an argument can be made that awareness of one's emotional associations provides the opportunity for some control over them.

Terms and phrases like the following are commonly used with examining emotional response objectives and tasks:

- What are your feelings about
- What is the logic underlying these feelings
- How reasonable is your thinking

The common format for examining emotional response tasks is short or extended written and oral constructed-response formats.

Examining Emotional Response With Information

Examining emotional response tasks for the domain of information involve identifying any emotions associated with details and organizing ideas and the logic behind these associations. For example, the first examining emotional response task for details involves facts regarding a specific political issue. Students are asked to identify any emotions associated with the political issue and

(Text continues on page 158)

Figure 8.3 Examining Emotion Objectives and Tasks

	Task	Objective	Knowledge Focus	Subject, Grade	Benchmark Statement
Information: Details: Terms, Facts, Time sequences	What emotions do you have, if any, about the sources of a specific political conflict that we have been studying, whether they are historical—such as those associated with slavery, with extending civil rights to all Americans—or more recent, such as immigration and the war in Iraq? What do you think gives rise to these emotions? Does your thinking make sense?	The student will be able to identify any emotions associated with a specific political issue and analyze the reasoning behind those emotions.	The details regarding a specific political issue	Civics 6–8	Knows about both past and present political conflicts in the United States (e.g., slavery, civil rights, suffrage, the role of religion in the U.S. government, events leading to the creation of the country and it's bicoastal expansion).
	What emotions, if any, do you have about specific human-caused changes that are taking place in different regions across the United States and what these changes might mean for the future? Select a specific change to react to. What kind of thinking on your part do these emotions suggest? How reasonable is your thinking?	The student will be able to identify any emotions associated with specific human-caused changes in different regions of the United States and analyze the reasoning behind those emotions.	The details regarding specific human-caused changes in different regions of the United States	Geography 3–5	Understands the potential impact that changes caused by humans can have on different regions (e.g., the reintroduction of wolves into wildlife preserves in Montana).
Information: Organizing Generalization	What emotions, if any, do you have about the fact that primary and secondary sources reflect the motives, interests and biases of their authors and may contradict each other? What thinking might give rise to these emotions? Is it logical?	The student will be able to identify any emotions associated with contradictions among primary and secondary sources and analyze the reasoning behind those emotions.	Generalizations about primary and secondary sources	Historical Understanding 7–8	Understands the motives, interests and possible biases in different primary and secondary sources (e.g., letters, photos, information from newspapers and magazines, eyewitness accounts or hearsay).

Figure 8.3 (Continued)

	Task	Objective	Knowledge Focus	Subject, Grade	Benchmark Statement
Information: Organizing Principle	What emotions, if any, do you have when you consider the concept of extinction? Do you consider it in terms of its importance in biological evolution, or do you think of it differently? Is your thinking logical? Why or why not?	The student will be able to identify any emotions associated with the concept of extinction and analyze the reasoning behind those emotions.	Principles regarding extinction	Science 6–8	Understands extinction and how important its effect on biological evolution is (e.g., when an environment changes, not all species are able to adapt; many of the species that have lived on the earth have suffered extinction).
Mental Procedure: Skill	What emotions, if any, do you have about asking questions in order to broaden a classroom discussion? What is the thinking behind this? Does your thinking make sense?	The student will be able to identify any emotions associated with asking questions in the classroom and analyze the reasoning behind those emotions.	The skill of asking questions in class	Language Arts 9–12	Enriches classroom discussions by asking questions.
	We have been practicing a technique for handling the stress of doing poorly on a class assignment. What emotions, if any, do you have about this strategy? What thinking gives rise to these emotions? How logical is that thinking?	The student will be able to identify any emotions associated with learning strategies for coping with the stress of doing poorly on a class assignment and examine the thinking behind those emotions.	The skill of coping with the stress of doing poorly on a class assignment	Health 6–8	Knows strategies for coping with the stress of doing poorly on a class assignment.
Mental Procedure: Process	What emotions, if any, do you associate with responding to questions and feedback after a presentation you have given—for example, clarifying and defending your ideas or expanding on a topic? What thinking gives rise to these emotions? Does it seem logical? Why or why not?	The student will be able to identify any emotions associated with seeking feedback to revise a presentation and analyze the logic behind those emotions.	The process of revising a presentation	Language Arts 9–12	Revises a presentation by responding to questions and feedback (e.g., elaborates on a topic, clarifies and defends ideas, uses logical arguments and logical organization, evaluates overall achievement, sets future goals).

	Task	Objective	Knowledge Focus	Subject, Grade	Benchmark Statement
	What emotions, if any, do you have when you are presented a problem situation that you must translate into another form—oral, written, concrete, or some other form? What is the logic behind these emotions? Does it make sense?	The student will be able to identify any emotions associated with translating a problem situation from one form into another and analyze the reasoning behind those emotions.	The process of translating a problem situation into various forms	Math 6–8	Uses oral, written, concrete, pictorial, and graphical forms to represent problem situations and translates among these forms.
Psychomotor Procedure: Skill	What emotions, if any, do you have about learning and mastering a specific advanced skill in your sport? What do you think causes these emotions? Is your thinking reasonable?	The student will be able to identify any emotions associated with learning and mastering advanced skills in a chosen sport and analyze the reasoning behind those emotions.	An advanced skill in a specific sport	Physical Education 9–12	Uses advanced skills associated with select sports or activities (e.g., swimming, dance, climbing, tennis, lacrosse).
	What emotions, if any, do you think of when you are required to parallel park in driver's education? What is the thinking behind these associations? Does your thinking make sense?	The student will be able to identify any emotions associated with learning to parallel park and analyze the reasoning behind those emotions.	The skill of parallel parking	Driver's Education 9–12	Applies the skills and processes for driving in a congested area.
Psychomotor Procedure: Process	Select one of the new sports we have been studying. What emotions, if any, do you have when you think about learning that sport? What is the reasoning behind your reaction?	The student will be able to identify any emotions associated with learning a new sport and analyze the thinking behind those emotions.	The process of learning a new sport	Physical Education 3–6	Improves physical performance by making use of information provided by both internal and external sources (e.g., self-assessment, peer, and coach review).
	What emotions, if any, do you associate with the process of producing an artwork that reflects your personal beliefs? What reasons are there for these associations? Do they make sense?	The student will be able to identify any emotions associated with producing an artwork and analyze the reasoning behind those emotions.	The process of producing a work of art	Visual Arts 9–12	Attempts to carry out personal intentions in artwork.

the reasoning behind these associations. The first examining emotional response task for organizing ideas involves emotional responses relative to generalizations about primary and secondary sources.

Examining Emotional Response With Mental Procedures

Examining emotional response tasks for the domain of mental procedures involve identifying emotions associated with mental skills and processes and the logic behind these associations. For example, the first examining emotional response task for mental skills addresses specific skills for asking questions in class. Here the teacher has provided students with a few question-asking techniques. Students are asked to identify emotions associated with these techniques and the logic behind these associations. The first examining emotional response task for mental processes involves emotional responses relative to the process of revising a presentation.

Examining Emotional Response With Psychomotor Procedures

Examining emotional response tasks for the domain of psychomotor procedures involve identifying emotions associated with psychomotor skills and processes and the logic behind these associations. For example, the first examining emotional response task for psychomotor skills addresses a specific advanced skill in a specific sport. Students identify any associated emotions and the logic behind these emotions. The first examining emotional response task for psychomotor processes involves emotional responses regarding the process of learning a new sport.

EXAMINING MOTIVATION

The final type of self-system thinking involves examining overall motivation to improve one's understanding of or competence in a specific type of knowledge. As described in Chapter 2, overall motivation is a composite of the other three aspects of self-system thinking: perceptions of importance, perceptions of efficacy, and emotional response. Examining motivation can be considered an "omnibus" self-system process incorporating the other three aspects of the self-system. Figure 8.4 lists objectives and tasks for examining motivation across the three knowledge domains.

Ideally, when students respond to tasks like those in Figure 8.4, they consider all three self-system components that can affect motivation. They comment on the importance they ascribe to the knowledge, the level of efficacy they perceive, and any emotions they associate with the knowledge. They also explain which of these three factors dominates their motivation. Of course the sophistication of students'

(Text continues on page 163)

Figure 8.4 Examining Motivation Objectives and Tasks

	Task	Objective	Knowledge Focus	Subject, Grade	Benchmark Statement
Information: Details: Terms, Facts, Time sequences	How interested are you in learning more about the location of your school, home, and state? Why are you interested or not interested? Are your reasons good reasons?	The student will be able to identify his or her level of motivation to increase understanding of the location of his or her school, home, and state.	Details about school, home, and state	Geography K–2	Locates familiar places, such as school, home, and neighborhood, as well as larger areas, such as one's own community, state, and country.
	Each of us has selected a different snack food to study. How interested are you in learning about the snack you have selected? Why do you have this level of interest? Does your thinking make sense?	The student will be able to identify his or her level of motivation to increase understanding of a specific type of snack food and provide some reasons for this perception.	Details about a specific snack food	Health 3–5	Understands how to practice healthful eating (e.g., eating vegetables rather than potato chips, eating a variety of nutritious foods, eating periodically throughout the day to assist energy levels and sustain growth).
Information: Organizing Generalization	Do you have an interest in learning how historical accounts can change, based on newly uncovered records and interpretations? Yes or no? Explain your reasoning. Does it make good sense? Why or why not?	The student will be able to identify his or her level of motivation to increase understanding of how historical accounts can change, based on new information, and analyze the reasoning for this level of motivation.	Generalizations about historical accounts	Historical Understanding 7–8	Knows that historical interpretations and accounts change, due to recently discovered documents or facts and changing politics.

(Continued)

Figure 8.4 (Continued)

	Task	Objective	Knowledge Focus	Subject, Grade	Benchmark Statement
Information: Organizing Principle	How would you describe your level of motivation for understanding how elements are arranged in the periodic table? Why do you think you are motivated this way? Is your thinking reasonable? Explain.	The student will be able to identify his or her level of motivation to increase understanding of how elements are arranged in the periodic table and analyze the reasoning for this level of motivation.	Principles regarding the periodic table	Science 9–12	Knows the arrangement of elements in the periodic table and knows that patterns appear within the table, illustrating elements with similar properties (e.g., numbers of protons, neutrons, and electrons; relationship between atomic number and atomic mass).
Mental Procedure: Skill	How interested are you in being good at following the rules of conversation we have been studying, like taking turns and raising your hand to speak in class? Why are you interested? Are there good reasons to be interested?	The student will be able to identify his or her level of motivation to increase competence in following the rules of conversation and provide some reasons for this thinking.	Specific rules of conversation	Language Arts K–2	Adheres to conventions of conversation and discussion (e.g., listens, takes turns, raises hand to speak, stays on topic).
	Are you motivated to be able to use a spreadsheet to update and add data? Why or why not? Does your thinking make sense?	The student will be able to identify his or her level of motivation to increase competence in using a spreadsheet to update and add data and analyze the logic of his or her thinking.	Updating and adding data to a spreadsheet	Technology 6–8	Uses a spreadsheet to make changes to data.

	Task	Objective	Knowledge Focus	Subject, Grade	Benchmark Statement
Mental Procedure: Process	What is your level of interest in being able to accurately use the conventions of Spanish we are studying, especially when it concerns using the right language for different settings, such as social and academic? Why? Are there good reasons behind your thinking?	The student will be able to identify his or her level of motivation to increase competence in using the conventions of Spanish and analyze the reasoning for this level of motivation.	The process of using the conventions of a foreign language during conversation	Foreign Language 5–8	Uses language mechanics, conventions and style (e.g., complex grammatical structures, slang, idioms, polite and informal forms and status indicators, vernacular dialects and diction) appropriate to social, academic and ceremonial audiences.
	How strongly are you motivated to be able to use the rectangular coordinate system to model and to solve problems? Why? How logical is your thinking? Explain.	The student will be able to identify his or her level of motivation to increase competence in using the rectangular coordinate system and analyze the reasoning for this level of motivation.	Using rectangular coordinates to solve problems	Math 6–8	Models and solves problems using the rectangular coordinate system.
Psychomotor Procedure: Skill	Do you want to learn the proper warm-up and cool-down exercises? What are your reasons? Are the reasons you have identified good reasons?	The student will be able to identify his or her level of motivation to increase competence in the use of warm-up and cool-down exercises and provide reasons for his or her thinking.	Warm-up and cool-down exercises	Physical Education 3–5	Knows how to properly warm up and cool down and knows why both are necessary.

(Continued)

Figure 8.4 (Continued)

	Task	Objective	Knowledge Focus	Subject, Grade	Benchmark Statement
	How motivated are you to increase your skill at using the brush strokes we have been studying? What reasons do you have for being this motivated? Do these reasons make good sense? Defend your position.	The student will be able to identify his or her level of motivation to increase competence in using particular brush strokes and analyze the reasoning for this level of motivation.	Specific brush strokes	Visual Arts 9–12	Carries out intentions in artwork using confidence and sensitivity as well as skill, technique, and process.
Psychomotor Procedure: Process	How interested are you in being able to read stories aloud smoothly and with good expression? Why do you think you are interested or not interested?	The student will be able to identify his or her level of motivation to increase competence in reading familiar stories aloud and analyze the reasoning for this level of motivation.	The process of reading a story aloud	Language Arts K–2	Fluently and expressively reads passages aloud from stories, poems, and assigned passages (e.g., reads with rhythm, flow, meter, tempo, pitch, tone, intonation).
	How would you describe your interest in being able to perform your instrument on pitch, in rhythm, and with an appropriate tempo? Why do you feel this way? Does your thinking make sense?	The student will be able to identify his or her level of motivation to increase competence in performing on a specific musical instrument and analyze the reasoning for this level of motivation.	Playing a musical instrument	Music 3–5	Performs with attention to pitch and rhythm and uses appropriate dynamics and timbre while maintaining a steady tempo.

responses is dependent on their age and maturity. Whereas older students might be expected to provide a detailed explanation of the factors affecting their motivation, primary students would be expected to provide a simple statement of their level of motivation and a basic reason or two for this perception.

Objectives and tasks for examining motivation are expressed in many ways, although common phrases include the following:

- How interested are you
- How motivated are you
- How would you explain your level of interest
- How reasonable is your thinking

The common format for examining motivation tasks is short or extended written and oral constructed response. Graphic organizers like that depicted in Figure 8.5 can be used by students to aid in their response to examining motivation tasks.

The graphic organizer in Figure 8.5 has a place for students to list their perceptions of importance, their perceptions of efficacy, and their perceptions of emotional response. This cues them to three major factors in motivation. There is also a section in the graphic organizer cueing them to explain how these three factors interact to enhance or decrease their motivation.

Figure 8.5   Graphic Organizer for Motivation

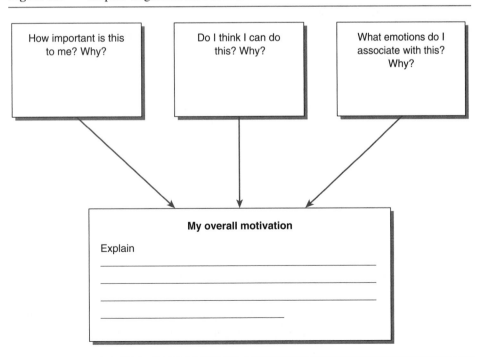

Examining Motivation With Information

Examining motivation tasks for the domain of information involve identifying one's level of motivation to learn details and organizing ideas and then analyzing the reasons for the identified level of motivation. For example, the first examining motivation task for details involves details about school, home, and state. Students must determine whether they are interested in learning about these details as well as the reasons for their identified level of motivation. The first examining motivation task for organizing ideas involves perceptions of motivation relative to generalizations about historical accounts.

Examining Motivation With Mental Procedures

Examining motivation tasks for the domain of mental procedures involve identifying one's level of motivation to learn mental skills and processes and then analyzing the reasons for the identified level of motivation. For example, the first examining motivation task for mental skills involves specific rules of conversation. Students must identify their interest in learning these rules and the reasons behind their level of interest. The first examining motivation task for mental processes involves perceptions of motivation relative to the process of using conventions in foreign language.

Examining Motivation With Psychomotor Procedures

Examining motivation tasks for the domain of psychomotor procedures involve identifying one's level of motivation to learn psychomotor skills and processes and then analyzing the reasons for the identified level of motivation. For example, the first examining motivation task for psychomotor skills involves specific warm-up and cool-down exercises. Students identify their level of motivation for learning these psychomotor skills and the reasons behind the identified level. The first examining motivation task for psychomotor processes involves perceptions of motivation relative to the process of reading a story aloud.

SUMMARY OF KEY POINTS FOR SELF-SYSTEM OBJECTIVES AND TASKS

Examining Importance Objectives and Tasks

- Require students to identify the extent to which they perceive learning specific knowledge to be important and analyze the logic of their perceptions
- Use terms and phrases like the following: how important is it to you, why do you think it might be important, can you provide some reason why it is important, how logical is your thinking
- Use short or extended written and oral constructed-response formats

Examining Efficacy Objectives and Tasks

- Require students to identify the extent to which they believe they can learn or get better at specific knowledge and analyze the logic of their beliefs
- Use terms and phrases like the following: can you improve, how well do you think you can do, how well can you learn, how good are you at, how logical is your thinking
- Use short or extended written and oral constructed-response formats

Examining Emotional Response Objectives and Tasks

- Require students to identify emotions associated with knowledge and analyze the logic behind these emotions
- Use terms and phrases like the following: what are your feelings about, what is the logic underlying your thinking, how reasonable is your thinking
- Use short and extended written and oral constructed-response formats

Examining Motivation Objectives and Tasks

- Require students to identify their level of motivation for learning specific types of knowledge and the logic behind the identified level of motivation. Ideally students include their perception of importance, efficacy, and emotional response in their analyses.
- Use terms and phrases like the following: how interested are you, how motivated are you, how would you explain your level of interest, how reasonable is your thinking
- Use short or extended written and oral constructed-response formats

CHAPTER NINE

The New Taxonomy as a Scale for Student Performance

The previous eight chapters have addressed objectives and tasks across the three domains of knowledge (information, mental procedures, and psychomotor procedures) for each of the six levels of the New Taxonomy. In effect the New Taxonomy represents a tacit scale of student performance. Objectives and assessment tasks could be designed across all six levels of the New Taxonomy for a knowledge component that is the focus of a particular unit of instruction or a particular grading period. To illustrate, assume that a district, school, or teacher has identified information about the solar system as the focus of instruction at the eighth grade. Figure 9.1 lists potential objectives and tasks regarding the solar system for all six levels of the New Taxonomy.

Figure 9.1 illustrates that it is possible to generate objectives and tasks for specific types of knowledge at a specific grade level for all six levels of the New Taxonomy. Here the knowledge focus is information about the solar system at the eighth grade. For each level of the New Taxonomy, specific objectives and sample tasks have been articulated. Using these guidelines, teachers could construct their own tasks or use those designed by the school or district to determine each student's position on the six levels of the New Taxonomy for this particular topic. This is probably not advisable for at least two reasons.

First, as described in the New Taxonomy (Marzano & Kendall, 2007), the metacognitive and self-system processes are meant to be addressed as an integral part of academic content. Unfortunately, this perception is not commonly shared throughout K–12 education. However, metacognitive and self-system skills are becoming accepted as a viable type of supporting or complimentary curriculum to academic content. We discuss this later in this chapter.

The second reason for not using all six levels of the New Taxonomy as a scale for measuring students is that within a school system, different grade levels focus on very different types of knowledge. For example, at the eighth-grade level, the expectation

Figure 9.1   Complete Articulation of New Taxonomy Regarding Information
Knowledge About the Solar System

New Taxonomy Level	Objective	Sample Task
Level 6— Self-System: Examining Motivation	The student will be able to analyze his or her motivation to learn about the solar system.	How would you describe your level of interest to learn more about the solar system? What are your reasons for this level of motivation? How logical is your thinking?
Level 5— Metacognition: Monitoring Clarity	The student will be able to identify aspects of the solar system about which he or she is not clear.	Identify something about the solar system about which you are confused. Develop a plan to clear up your confusion.
Level 4— Knowledge Utilization: Investigating	The student will be able to investigate the gradual growth of knowledge about the solar system.	Select one of the current discoveries about the solar system we have studied in class. Investigate how the discovery came about and how it changed our thinking about the solar system.
Level 3— Analysis: Matching	The student will be able to identify similarities and differences between various planets in the solar system.	Identify two planets in our solar system and compare them on two or more characteristics of your choice.
Level 2— Comprehension: Integrating	The student will be able to explain the critical features of the solar system.	Explain what you consider to be the most important features of our solar system in terms of understanding how it operates.
Level 1— Retrieval: Recognizing and Recalling	The student will be able to recognize and recall important details about the solar system.	Briefly explain the following terms: • Planetary rings • Light year • Astronomical unit Determine if the following statements are true or false: 1. The path of objects traveling around the sun follows a law of planetary motion discovered by German astronomer Johannes Kepler in the early 1600s. 2. There are seventy-three known moons in the solar system. 3. Jupiter is a dwarf planet. 4. The term *celestial object* does not include earth. 5. Mercury has fifteen planetary rings. 6. The moon is about one-third the size of earth. 7. Venus is the coldest planet in the solar system. 8. Astronomers most often measure distances within the solar system in astronomical units.

for students might be that they can analyze information about the topic of the solar system—in the parlance of the New Taxonomy, the expectation is that students demonstrate competence in matching, classifying, analyzing errors, generalizing, and specifying regarding information about the solar system. At the fifth-grade level, the expectation might be that students can comprehend the important characteristics of the solar system—in New Taxonomy terms, the expectation is that they demonstrate competence in integrating and symbolizing information about the solar system. At the third-grade level, the expectation might be that students can retrieve basic information about the solar system—they can recognize and recall basic facts about the solar system. Thus it would be impractical and unwise to expect students to exhibit all levels of the New Taxonomy for all topics at each grade level. For measurement purposes, what is needed is a flexible scale that can translate the New Taxonomy into reasonable expectations and be easily used by teachers to design and score assessments.

A FLEXIBLE SCALE TO USE WITH THE NEW TAXONOMY

In a series of works, Marzano (2006; Marzano & Haystead, 2008) has a developed a scale that can be used to design and score assessments based on the first four levels of the New Taxonomy. That scale is depicted in Figure 9.2.

Figure 9.2   Scale for Use With the First Four Levels of the New Taxonomy

Score 4.0: In addition to Score 3.0 performance, in-depth inferences and applications that go beyond what was taught.
Score 3.5: In addition to Score 3.0 performance, partial success at inferences and applications that go beyond what was taught.
Score 3.0: No major errors or omissions regarding any of the information and/or processes (simple or complex) that were explicitly taught.
Score 2.5. No major errors or omissions regarding the simpler details and processes and partial knowledge of the more complex ideas and processes.
Score 2.0: No major errors or omissions regarding the simpler details and processes but major errors or omissions regarding the more complex ideas and processes.
Score 1.5: Partial knowledge of the simpler details and processes but major errors or omissions regarding the more complex ideas and processes.
Score 1.0: With help, a partial understanding of some of the simpler details and processes and some of the more complex ideas and processes.
Score 0.5: With help, a partial understanding of some of the simpler details and processes but not the more complex ideas and processes.
Score 0.0: Even with help, no understanding or skill demonstrated.

The scale in Figure 9.2 is generic. It is intended to be rewritten for specific grade level expectations using the New Taxonomy. To illustrate, assume that at fifth grade students are expected to comprehend the critical characteristics of the solar system. That is, the stated objective for fifth grade students is this: "The student will be able to explain the critical characteristics of the solar system." This expectation would be placed at score 3.0 in the scale. To determine score level 2.0, one simply moves down one level of the New Taxonomy. In effect the objective for score level 2.0 would be, "The student will be able to recall important details about the solar system." To determine score level 4.0, one moves up one level in the New Taxonomy. In effect, the objective for score level 4.0 would be, "The student will be able to analyze information about the solar system." As discussed, below score 4.0, objectives are more general in nature. With these three reference points identified, a scale specific to the topic of the solar system for the fifth grade can be written. This is depicted in Figure 9.3.

Figure 9.3 is a scale written specifically for the fifth-grade target objectives for the solar system. Note that for score 3.0 and 2.0, rather specific guidance is provided that allows teachers to generate and score assessments. We address this in the next section. Score value 4.0 is less specific because it involves inferences and applications that go beyond what was directly taught in class. Here teachers are provided guidance as to the type of inferences and applications students are expected to make. In this case, those inferences and applications address the analysis processes of the New Taxonomy.

Now consider a different grade level using the same general content—the solar system. Assume that at third grade, the target objective is that students will be able to retrieve important information about the solar system. Again this would occupy score 3.0 on the scale. To define score 2.0, one would move down a level on the New Taxonomy. However, retrieval is the lowest level of the New Taxonomy. In such cases, one looks for a hierarchic structure within a given taxonomic level. In this case, recognition is a lower level than recall. Recall then, is the expectation at score value 3.0; recognition is the expectation at score value 2.0. To define score value 4.0, one moves up one level in the New Taxonomy, to comprehension. Again a specific scale would be written. This is depicted in Figure 9.4.

This scale, although on the same general topic as that depicted in Figure 9.3, is quite different in that score values 2.0, 3.0 and 4.0 involve recognition, recall, and integration, respectively, whereas in Figure 9.3, score values 2.0, 3.0 and 4.0 involve recall, integration and analysis, respectively.

As the foregoing examples illustrate, when a grade-level statement of student expectations is specific enough to be placed on the New Taxonomy, a scale can be constructed using the generic scale in Figure 9.2. The grade-level expectation is placed in score value 3.0. Score value 2.0 is defined using one level down in the

Figure 9.3   Scale for the Topic of the Solar System at the Fifth Grade

Score 4.0	**In addition to score 3.0, in-depth inferences and applications that involve identifying implied similarities and differences, classifying, analyzing errors, generalizing, and specifying.**
Score 3.5	In addition to score 3.0 performance, in-depth inferences and applications with partial success.
Score 3.0	**While engaged in tasks that address the topic of the solar system, the student demonstrates comprehension of critical characteristics of the solar system, such as** • Basic interactions between the sun and planets in the solar system (e.g., explains why the planets stay in orbit around the sun) • Basic distinctions between the sun and planets in the solar system (e.g., shape, size, characteristics of rings, characteristics of moons, distance from the sun) **The student exhibits no major errors or omissions.**
Score 2.5	No major errors or omissions regarding the score 2.0 elements and partial knowledge of the score 3.0 elements.

Score 2.0	**No major errors or omissions regarding the simpler details and processes, such as**
	
	• Recalling specific terminology, such as
	   o Planetary rings
	   o Light-year
	   o Astronomical unit
	• Recalling isolated details, such as
	   o The moon is about one-third the size of earth.
	   o Astronomers most often measure distances within the solar system in astronomical units.
	   o Objects around the sun travel according to a law of planetary motion discovered by German astronomer Johannes Kepler in the early 1600s.
	   o The term *celestial object* does not include earth.
	
	However, the student exhibits major errors or omissions with score 3.0 elements.

Score 1.5	Partial knowledge of the score 2.0 elements but major errors or omissions regarding the score 3.0 elements.
Score 1.0	**With help, a partial understanding of some of the score 2.0 elements and some of the score 3.0 elements.**
Score 0.5	With help, a partial understanding of some of the score 2.0 elements but not the score 3.0 elements.
Score 0.0	**Even with help, no understanding or skill demonstrated.**

New Taxonomy and score value 4.0 is defined using one level up on the New Taxonomy. When recall is the focus of score value 3.0, recognition is used as the focus of score value 2.0.

Figure 9.4   Scale for the Topic of the Solar System at the Third Grade

Score 4.0	In addition to score 3.0, in-depth inferences and applications that involve identifying critical versus noncritical aspects of the solar system.
Score 3.5	In addition to score 3.0 performance, in-depth inferences and applications with partial success.
Score 3.0	While engaged in tasks that address the topic of the solar system, the student demonstrates recall of important information about the solar system, such as • There are eight planets in our solar system. • The earth is the third planet from the sun. • The earth is assumed to be the only planet that supports life. • There are many solar systems in the universe. • There are four gas giant planets in our solar system. • There are three dwarf planets in our solar system. • There are four inner planets and four outer planets in our solar system. **The student exhibits no major errors or omissions.**
Score 2.5	No major errors or omissions regarding the score 2.0 elements and partial knowledge of the score 3.0 elements.
Score 2.0	No major errors or omissions regarding the simpler details and processes, such as • Recognizing isolated details, such as 　○ Our planet is called Earth. 　○ The sun is a star. 　○ Each planet orbits the sun. 　○ Mercury is the name of the planet closest to the sun. 　○ Earth is the only planet with just one moon. **However, the student exhibits major errors or omissions with score 3.0 elements.**
Score 1.5	Partial knowledge of the score 2.0 elements but major errors or omissions regarding the score 3.0 elements.
Score 1.0	With help, a partial understanding of some of the score 2.0 elements and some of the score 3.0 elements.
Score 0.5	With help, a partial understanding of some of the score 2.0 elements but not the score 3.0 elements.
Score 0.0	Even with help, no understanding or skill demonstrated.

DESIGNING AND SCORING ASSESSMENTS

Once a scale has been constructed for a grade-level expectation, assessments can be constructed and scored. Again consider the scale in Figure 9.4. There recognition is the focus of score value 2.0. Based on the scale, the teacher can design recognition items like the following:

Determine if the following statements are true or false:

- The sun orbits Earth.
- Mercury appears blue when viewed through a telescope.
- Saturn has rings.
- Earth is between Venus and Mars.
- We live on the third planet from the Sun.

These true–false items are recognition items because students are provided with statements about the solar system and must recognize whether each statement is correct. Forced-choice items, like true–false, matching, and multiple choice, are commonly used for recognition items. (For a detailed discussion of common recognition items, see Marzano, 2006.)

The focus of score value 3.0 is recall. The teacher might design items like the following for score value 3.0:

Briefly answer the following:

- What are the different planets in the solar system? Start from the sun and identify each planet from the first to the last.
- Pick three planets and describe some of the important things we've learned about each.

Recall items require students to produce accurate information as opposed to simply recognizing it when it is provided. Consequently, recall items typically use short constructed-response formats. (For a discussion, see Chapter 3.)

The focus of score value 4.0 is integration. Here students must distinguish between critical versus noncritical elements for a given topic. An item like the following would elicit this type of thinking:

We have learned about earth's ability to support life. Pick three characteristics we have studied and explain why they are critical to support life on earth.

Here students must go beyond simply recalling information that has been taught. They must explain why certain characteristics are important to a specific phenomenon—the ability of earth to support life.

The three types of items generated by the teacher would be put together to form the assessment depicted in Figure 9.5.

To score the assessment in Figure 9.5, a teacher would first address each item and determine if a student's response received full credit (possibly signified by +), no credit (possibly signified by 0), or partial credit (possibly signified by *P*). The teacher then examines the pattern of response across score 2.0, 3.0 and 4.0 items and tasks. To understand how best to interpret response patterns, it is useful to begin with the score value of 3.0.

Figure 9.5   Assessment Based on Third-Grade Scale for the Solar System

Section I: For each item, identify whether it is true or false: 1. The sun orbits Earth. 2. Mercury appears blue when viewed through a telescope. 3. Saturn has rings. 4. Earth is between Venus and Mars. 5. We live on the third planet from the sun.
Section II: Briefly answer the following: 1. What are the different planets in the solar system? Start from the sun and identify each planet from the first to the last. 2. Pick three planets and describe some of the important things we've learned about each.
Section III: We have learned about earth's ability to support life. Pick three characteristics we have studied and explain why they are critical to support life on earth.

- A score of 3.0 indicates that a student has answered all items or tasks correctly that involve simpler details and processes (all score 2.0 items and tasks) **as well as** all items and tasks that involve more complex ideas and processes that were explicitly taught (all score 3.0 items and tasks). In effect, the score of 3.0 is the fulcrum of the scale. It represents the instructional goal for a specific topic.

- A score of 2.0 indicates that the student has answered all items and tasks correctly that involve simpler details and processes (all score 2.0 items and tasks), but has missed all items and tasks that involve more complex ideas and processes (all score 3.0 items and tasks).

- If a student has answered all items and tasks correctly regarding simpler details and processes (score 2.0 items and tasks) and **some** items and tasks correctly involving more complex ideas and processes (score 3.0 items and tasks) or has received **partial credit** on those items and tasks, a score of 2.5 is assigned.

- A score of 1.5 is assigned if a student receives partial credit on the score 2.0 items and tasks but misses all other types of items.

- A score of 1.0 is assigned if a student misses all items and tasks on an assessment but with help from the teacher demonstrates partial credit on the score 2.0 and score 3.0 items and tasks.

- A score of 0.5 is assigned if the student misses all items and tasks but with help demonstrates partial credit on the score 2.0 items and tasks (but does not demonstrate partial credit on the score 3.0 items and tasks).

- A score of 0.0 indicates that even with help, the student cannot answer any items or perform any tasks correctly.

- At the top end of the scale, a score of 4.0 is assigned if a student answers all items and tasks correctly (score 4.0 items and tasks, score 3.0 items and tasks, and score 2.0 items and tasks).

- A score of 3.5 is assigned if a student answers score 2.0 and score 3.0 items and tasks correctly and receives partial credit on score 4.0 items and tasks.

To illustrate, assume that a particular student answered all items correctly in Sections I and II of the assessment depicted in Figure 9.5 but did not answer the item in Section III correctly. The student would receive a score of 3.0 on the assessment. Had the student received partial credit on the items in Section III, his or her score would have been 3.5. If the student had answered all items correctly in Section I and answered some of the items correctly in Section II or received partial credit on some of these items, he or she would have received a score of 2.5. If the student answered no items correctly on the assessment but upon a discussion with the teacher was able to partially answer some questions in Section I and Section II with prompting, the student's score would be 1.0. For a more detailed discussion of various types of score patterns see Marzano (2006).

One of the advantages to scoring assessments using the scale presented in this chapter is that it is particularly useful in tracking student progress over time. To illustrate, consider Figure 9.6.

Figure 9.6   Tracking Student Progress

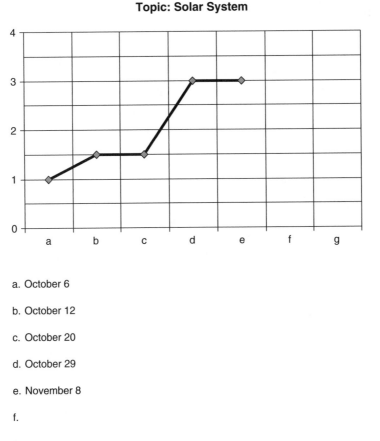

Topic: Solar System

a. October 6

b. October 12

c. October 20

d. October 29

e. November 8

f.

g.

Figure 9.6 depicts five scores for a particular student over time on the topic of the solar system. Assume that all assessments were similar to that shown in Figure 9.5. The student's scores have been graphed by the teacher and the student. This allows the teacher and student to examine growth over time. This particular student started with a score of 1.0—the student answered no questions on the test without help, but with help was able to receive partial credit on some score 2.0 and 3.0 items. By the fourth and fifth assessments, the student was able to independently answer score 2.0 and 3.0 items thus receiving a score of 3.0 on both assessments. Marzano (2006) has demonstrated how this type of graphing of student progress fulfills some of the defining features of formative assessment. It allows students to see their growth over time and provides assessment information about status at a particular point in time.

THE UNIQUE ROLE OF METACOGNITIVE AND SELF-SYSTEM PROCESSES

It is certainly possible to incorporate metacognitive and self-system processes into a scale like those depicted in Figure 9.3 and 9.4. Indeed if score 3.0 on a scale focuses on a knowledge utilization process such as investigation, it would make logical sense for score value 4.0 to address a metacognitive process like examining accuracy or examining clarity. And if score value 3.0 on a scale focuses on a metacognitive process such as examining accuracy or examining clarity, it would make logical sense for score value 4.0 to address a self-system process like examining motivation. This notwithstanding, K–12 educators typically want to isolate academic content as the centerpiece of the curriculum. This is evidenced by the current emphasis on national and state academic standards (for a discussion, see Marzano and Haystead, 2008). Consequently, districts and schools might reasonably elect to consider the metacognitive and self-system processes as a separate type of curriculum. This is in keeping with current discussions of personal and social skills. There is growing evidence that when such a curriculum is combined with a sound academic curriculum, students benefit both in terms of learning academic content as well as learning personal and social skills. Specifically, a meta-analysis by Durlak and Weissberg (2007) indicates that when skills like those in the metacognitive and self-system components of the New Taxonomy are taught in tandem with academic skills, both can be enhanced. They explain that "the association between academic performance and personal and social development is of great interest to educators, researchers, and policy makers" (p. 18). It should be noted that Durlak and Weissberg define personal and social development in a much broader manner than we define metacognition and self-system thinking; however, an examination of the types of skills they consider within their framework of personal and social development demonstrates that many of their personal skills are closely related to what we refer to in the later two categories of the New Taxonomy.

According to Durlak and Weissberg (2007), one important aspect of teaching metacognitive and self-system skills (i.e., personal skills) is to provide students with explicit models and practice in those skills. They note,

> New skill cannot be acquired immediately. It takes time and effort to develop new behaviors and often more complicated skills must be broken down into smaller steps and sequentially mastered. Therefore, a coordinated sequence of activities is required that links the learning steps and provides youth with opportunities to connect these steps. (p. 10)

In terms of the metacognitive and self-system processes listed in the New Taxonomy, these findings imply that teachers should teach specific strategies for metacognitive and self-systems skills. Consider, for example, the metacognitive process of specifying goals. To use this process as a supportive structure for learning content, teachers should provide students with explicit guidance in how to set concrete, measurable goals and how to design explicit plans that include time lines, resources and milestones. This is consistent with current discussions regarding enhancing student thinking. For example, Swartz, Costa, Beyer, Reagan, and Kallick (2008) discuss teaching students how to climb the "ladder of metacognition" (p. 99) as a critical aspect of teaching thinking. They also recommend teaching students how to gain control of their emotions and thought processes as a form of higher order thinking. Of course, these two components are similar to metacognitive and self-system thinking in the New Taxonomy.

In addition to learning strategies for metacognitive and self-system thinking, we believe students should keep track of their progress on these skills using a scale patterned after the generic scale in Figure 9.2. To illustrate, consider Figure 9.7.

Figure 9.7 is designed for the metacognitive skill of specifying goals at the high school level. Scales at the lower grade levels would necessarily be different to reflect differences in sophistication of expectations for this competency. Note that the score values 3.0 and 2.0 are spelled out for teachers. This provides guidance for instruction and assessment. That is, the scale communicates to high school teachers that they must explicitly teach the following:

- Strategies for setting specific learning goals with concrete ways to determine when they are attained
- Strategies for designing explicit plans for completing the goals with clear milestones along the way
- Strategies for identifying necessary resources and how the those resources will be acquired

Using the scale in Figure 9.7, students might systematically rate themselves. The teacher might also provide a rating. In addition to comparing teacher and student ratings, this system could be used to reinforce progress in the skill of specifying goals and celebrate that progress.

Figure 9.7   High School Scale for Specifying Goals

	Specifying Goals	
	High School (Grades 9–12)	
Score 4.0	**In addition to score 3.0 performance, in-depth inferences and applications that go beyond what was taught.**	
	Score 3.5	In addition to score 3.0 performance, in-depth inferences and applications with partial success.
Score 3.0	**While engaged in the metacognitive skills of specifying goals, the student exhibits the following behaviors:** • Identifies a specific learning goal with an concrete way to determine when it is attained • Identifies an explicit plan for completing the goal with clear milestones along the way • Identifies necessary resources and how those resources will be acquired The student exhibits no major errors or omissions.	
	Score 2.5	No major errors or omissions regarding the score 2.0 elements and partial knowledge of the score 3.0 elements.
Score 2.0	**The student is successful with the simpler details and behaviors such as** • Identifies a goal but the does not identify a concrete way to determine when it is attained • Identifies an explicit plan for completing the goal but does not include milestones • Identifies necessary resources but does not identify how those resources will be acquired **However, the student exhibits major errors or omissions with score 3.0 elements.**	
	Score 1.5	Partial knowledge of the score 2.0 elements but major errors or omissions regarding the score 3.0 elements.
Score 1.0	**With help, a partial understanding of some of the score 2.0 elements and some of the score 3.0 elements.**	
	Score 0.5	With help, a partial understanding of some of the score 2.0 but not the score 3.0 elements.
Score 0.0	**Even with help, no understanding or skill demonstrated.**	

Afterword

In this handbook, we have provided district, school, and classroom educators with a practical guide to designing and assessing educational objectives using *The New Taxonomy of Educational Objectives* (Marzano & Kendall, 2007). Without a sound theoretical base, objectives and their assessments become subjective and ultimately ineffectual. Where *The New Taxonomy of Educational Objectives* provides the theory and research base to design objectives and their related assessments, this handbook describes precisely how to go about designing those objectives and assessments. It is our hope that educators use this handbook to rethink and restructure their standards, assessments, and curriculum. We acknowledge that the New Taxonomy and this handbook cannot address all issues regarding standards, assessments, and curriculum for individual districts, schools and classrooms. Consequently we encourage educators to make the necessary adaptations and alterations in the New Taxonomy to meet their specific needs.

References

Airasian, P. W. (1994). The impact of the Taxonomy on testing and evaluation. In L. W. Anderson & L. A. Sosniak (Eds.), *Bloom's Taxonomy: A forty-year retrospective: Ninety-third yearbook of the National Society for the Study of Education* (pp. 82–102). Chicago: University of Chicago Press.

Anderson, L. W., Krathwohl, D. R., Airasian, P. W., Cruikshank, K. A., Mayer, R. E., Pintrich, P. R., et al. (Eds.). (2001). *A taxonomy for learning, teaching, and assessing: A revision of Bloom's taxonomy of educational objectives.* New York: Longman.

Bloom, B. S., Engelhart, M. D., Furst, E. J., Hill, W. H., & Krathwohl, D. R. (Eds.). (1956). *Taxonomy of educational objectives: The classification of educational goals. Handbook I: Cognitive domain.* New York: David McKay.

Durlak, J. A., & Weissberg, R. P. (2007). *The impact of after-school programs promote personal and social skills.* Chicago: Collaborative for Academic, Social, and Emotional Learning.

Hyerle, D. (1996). *Visual tools for constructing knowledge.* Alexandria, VA: Association for Supervision and Curriculum Development.

Marzano, R. J. (2006). *Classroom assessment & grading that work.* Alexandria, VA: Association for Supervision and Curriculum Development.

Marzano, R. J. (2007). *The art and science of teaching: A comprehensive framework for effective instruction.* Alexandria, VA: Association for Supervision and Curriculum Development.

Marzano, R. J., & Haystead, M. W. (2008). *Making standards useful in the classroom.* Alexandria, VA: Association for Supervision and Curriculum Development.

Marzano, R. J., & Kendall, J. S. (2007). *The new taxonomy of educational objectives* (2nd ed.). Thousand Oaks, CA: Corwin Press.

Marzano, R. J., & Pickering, D. J. (2005). *Building academic vocabulary: Teacher's manual.* Alexandria, VA: Association for Supervision and Curriculum Development.

Swartz, R. J., Costa, A. L., Beyer, B. K., Reagan, R., & Kallick, B. (2007). *Thinking-based learning: Activating students' potential.* Norwood, MA: Christopher-Gordon.

Index

CORWIN PRESS

The Corwin Press logo—a raven striding across an open book—represents the union of courage and learning. Corwin Press is committed to improving education for all learners by publishing books and other professional development resources for those serving the field of PreK–12 education. By providing practical, hands-on materials, Corwin Press continues to carry out the promise of its motto: **"Helping Educators Do Their Work Better."**

American Association of School Administrators

The American Association of School Administrators, founded in 1865, is the professional organization for over 13,000 educational leaders across America. AASA's mission is to support and develop effective school system leaders who are dedicated to the highest quality public education for all children.

NATIONAL ASSOCIATION OF ELEMENTARY SCHOOL PRINCIPALS
Serving All Elementary and Middle Level Principals

The 29,500 members of the National Association of Elementary School Principals provide administrative and instructional leadership for public and private elementary and middle schools throughout the United States, Canada, and overseas. Founded in 1921, NAESP is today a vigorously independent professional association with its own headquarters building in Alexandria, Virginia, just across the Potomac River from the nation's capital. From this special vantage point, NAESP conveys the unique perspective of the elementary and middle school principal to the highest policy councils of our national government. Through national and regional meetings, award-winning publications, and joint efforts with its 50 state affiliates, NAESP is a strong advocate both for its members and for the 33 million American children enrolled in preschool, kindergarten, and grades 1 through 8.

NATIONAL ASSOCIATION OF SECONDARY SCHOOL
PRINCIPALS

Promoting Excellence in School Leadership

The National Association of Secondary School Principals—promoting excellence in school leadership since 1916—provides its members the professional resources to serve as visionary leaders. NASSP further promote sstudent leadership development through its sponsorship of the National Honor Society®, the National Junior Honor Society®, and the National Association of Student Councils®. For more information, visit www.principals.org.